THE WIDE BRIM

The Florida History and Culture Series

Florida A&M University, Tallahassee
Florida Atlantic University, Boca Raton
Florida Gulf Coast University, Ft. Myers
Florida International University, Miami
Florida State University, Tallahassee
University of Central Florida, Orlando
University of Florida, Gainesville
University of North Florida, Jacksonville
University of South Florida, Tampa
University of West Florida, Pensacola

University Press of Florida

Gainesville · Tallahassee · Tampa · Boca Raton · Pensacola
Orlando · Miami · Jacksonville · Ft. Myers

THE WIDE BRIM

Early Poems and
Ponderings of

Marjory Stoneman Douglas

Edited by Jack E. Davis

All photographs, unless otherwise noted, courtesy of the Florida State
Archives. Chapter 2 photograph courtesy of Archives and Special
Collections Department, Richter Library, University of Miami

Columns reprinted with permission of the *Miami Herald*

07 06 05 04 03 02 6 5 4 3 2 1

Library of Congress Cataloging-in-Publication Data
Douglas, Marjory Stoneman.
The wide brim: early poems and ponderings of Marjory
Stoneman Douglas / edited by Jack E. Davis.
p. cm.—(The Florida history and culture series)
ISBN 0-8130-2458-7 (cloth: alk. paper)
1. Florida—Poetry. 2. Florida. I. Davis, Jack E., 1956–. II. Title. III. Series.
PS3554.O8275 W53 2002
811'.54—dc21 2001054023

The University Press of Florida is the scholarly publishing agency for the
State University System of Florida, comprising Florida A&M University,
Florida Atlantic University, Florida Gulf Coast University, Florida
International University, Florida State University, University of Central
Florida, University of Florida, University of North Florida, University of
South Florida, and University of West Florida.

University Press of Florida
15 Northwest 15th Street
Gainesville, FL 32611-2079
http://www.upf.com

Contents

Foreword

The Wide Brim: Early Poems and Ponderings of Marjory Stoneman Douglas is the nineteenth volume of a series devoted to the study of Florida history and culture. During the past half century, the burgeoning population and increased national and international visibility of Florida have sparked a great deal of popular interest in the state's past, present, and future. As the favorite destination of countless tourists and as the new home for millions of retirees and other migrants, modern Florida has become a demographic, political, and cultural bellwether. But, unfortunately, the quantity and quality of the literature on Florida's distinctive heritage and character have not kept pace with the Sunshine State's enhanced status. In an effort to remedy this situation—to provide an accessible and attractive format for the publication of Florida-related books—the University Press of Florida has established the Florida History and Culture series.

As coeditors of the series, we are committed to the creation of an eclectic but carefully crafted set of books that will provide the field of Florida studies with a new focus and that will encourage Florida researchers and writers to consider the broader implications and context of their work. The series will include standard academic monographs, works of synthesis, memoirs, and anthologies. And, while the series will feature books of historical interest, we encourage authors researching Florida's environment, politics, literature, and popular or material culture to submit their manuscripts for inclusion in the series. We want each book to retain a distinct "personality" and voice, but at the same time we hope to foster a sense of community and collaboration among Florida scholars.

The Wide Brim, Jack E. Davis's carefully edited volume of Marjory Stoneman Douglas's early writing in the *Miami Herald,* offers readers a new look at modern Florida's most celebrated environmental writer. Those who

have marveled at the elegant prose and insightful commentary of Douglas's 1947 classic *The Everglades: River of Grass* will find the same qualities in the poems and essays collected in *The Wide Brim*. Framed by Davis's comprehensive introduction and headnotes, the selections from Douglas's column The Galley represent the full range of her abiding interest in human affairs, natural history, and the state of Florida, her adopted home.

Born in Minnesota in 1890, Douglas later lived in the Northeast before moving to Miami in 1915. Joining her father, Frank Stoneman, the editor of the *Miami Herald,* who hired her as a reporter and society editor, she soon demonstrated her talents as a feature writer and social critic. Following a two-year hiatus while she worked for the Red Cross in Europe, she returned to the *Herald* in March 1920 to write a daily column entitled The Galley Proof (later shortened to simply The Galley). For the next three years, her prose and verse provided boom-era Miamians with a shrewd look at the rapidly changing world of South Florida and postwar America. Few items subject to comment escaped her subtle notice, and, despite the grind of turning out a daily column, she rarely failed to present fresh commentary on everything from local politics to human nature itself. Jack Davis's broad sampling of her more than one thousand columns captures the passionate spirit and searching intelligence of this remarkable woman. No one who reads Douglas's words can come away from the experience without appreciating her deep commitment to intellectual inquiry and reflective thought. Neglected and all but forgotten for three-quarters of a century, the literary treasures gathered together in *The Wide Brim* give new life to one of Florida's most nimble minds. Put on your reading glasses, pour yourself a glass of sweet tea, put on your own wide brim, and enjoy.

Raymond Arsenault and Gary R. Mormino
Series Editors

Acknowledgments

Editing a book of this type has meant reassembling another person's work in a coherent form that fairly reflects that person's life. Successful assembly in this case required the help of others, who assisted with capital expenditure, blueprint reading, and design recommendations. Yet any poorly fitted parts resulted from my own faulty measures and any surface dings from my hammer alone.

A faculty research grant from the graduate school of the University of Alabama at Birmingham covered the cost of travel and photocopying. I am grateful to Tobie Muir and George Rosner for allowing me access to the Marjory Stoneman Douglas papers at the University of Miami, where Bill Brown and Marcia Evanson with unfailing courtesy facilitated my research in the Archives and Special Collections Department. Ray Mohl, who conceived the idea for this project, Karen Utz, Pamela Valentine, Jane Morgan, Kathy Arsenault, Ray Arsenault, Melissa Seixas, Eileen Moore, and Rachel Epstein gave sage advice on presenting and organizing the book's contents. The "anonymous" readers—Carl Hiaasen, Suzan Harrison, and Michael P. Branch—deserve thanks for offering valuable suggestions on the original draft that have made the book more accessible to readers. Sonya Rudenstine helped me enormously with her close scrutiny of the text and her sharp eye for style and misguided interpretations. Thank you, Yank.

Finally, the important work in this volume originated eight decades ago at the desk of the late Marjory Stoneman Douglas. While conducting research for a larger project on Douglas, I struck fortune when I came upon her all-but-forgotten newspaper column, The Galley. She is appreciated here for the legacy of her wit, insight, and provocativeness that add texture to life today and that made collecting her writings for this volume enjoyable and rewarding.

Jack E. Davis

THE WIDE BRIM

The Florida History and Culture Series

At a dedication ceremony in Tallahassee, at which
the Florida Department of Natural Resources build-
ing was named in Douglas's honor, April 1981. Cour-
tesy of Florida State Archives.

Introduction

She wore a hat for the day's special event, as she did for all such events, even though fashion of the 1980s dictated otherwise. Angled against the Florida sun, the hat's broad, floating brim was like a halo. It was a curious image of someone whose life seemed endless. She was in fact immortalized that very afternoon in April, the month of her ninety-first birthday, when the state dedicated its new Department of Natural Resources building in her name. At the moment of honor, a corps of press photographers snapped her picture as she threw an arm up in a triumphant gesture of celebration. When her time came to speak, the whirring cameras followed her to a lectern that towered before her diminished frame. She reached up and held each side like the shoulders of a dance partner, although she was never one to follow another's lead. Her voice was inconceivably strong and authoritative. What the cameras could not capture was the crucial contradiction between her physical antiquity and her invincible presence. Although she was reserved that day, her usual fashion was to scold and berate public officials whenever she discussed her most beloved cause. Just because lawmakers had named a building for her, she gently admonished those present that day, did not mean she would blindly support their future policies.[1]

The caveat was typical of Marjory Stoneman Douglas. The public knew her as an outspoken and constant crusader for Everglades protection. Journalists exalted her to the heights of royalty and even sainthood, and they made a game of trying to attach to her the perfect Everglades-related sobriquet. "Our Lady of the Glades," "Grand Dame of the Everglades," "Guardian of the Glades," "Guardian of the Glades' Spirit," "First Lady of the Everglades," "Empress of the Everglades," "Champion of the Everglades," and "Everglades Evangelist" were some of their creations. One newspaper writer noted, "History has not yet decided whether she should

be called the Grand Dame, the First Lady, the Mother or the Grandmother of the Everglades."[2] To know the woman with the wide-brim hat in the last few decades was indeed to know the Everglades. She was one of Florida's most impassioned environmentalists, a sage among nature's lovers, and among nature's enemies, a busybody of an old lady.

But to regard Marjory Stoneman Douglas simply as a committed environmentalist is to behold a single-hued image like that of the photograph. She was a person of considerable depth whose life stretched to 108 years, from 1890 to 1998. Not until 1969, when she was approaching her ninth decade, did she actually give her full time to Everglades preservation and restoration. Her devotion to human causes—women's suffrage, the poor, child welfare, and civil liberties—long preceded her environmental work. Early in life, she absorbed the Quaker morality of her father and paternal ancestors, and from her professors at college she learned about society's many injustices. She faced her own share of hardships—her mother's mental illness and death, her parents' divorce, and her own unfortunate and short-lived marriage—before reaching early adulthood.[3] Although she never compared her problems to those of the dispossessed, her personal experiences, combined with her well-groomed value system, encouraged her to try to improve society. She did so by putting pen to paper.

This volume is about Douglas the socially conscious writer, more specifically Douglas the newspaper columnist and poet. For more than three years in the early 1920s, she wrote a daily column, which often included her own poetry, of social and political commentary for the *Miami Herald*. She spent nearly ten years as a newspaper writer, from 1915 to 1923, interrupted by a short stint as a correspondent for the Red Cross immediately after World War I. For Douglas, the column represented valuable training ground for a long career in writing, one of the longest in American letters. For the reader of this volume, her columns offer a glimpse into her life and the personality beyond the sawgrass.

Before she was anything else, Douglas was a writer. She spent her entire adult life shaping a writing career for herself, first as a journalist, then as a short-story writer, and later as an author of fiction and nonfiction books. The work that defined her as a public figure was *The Everglades: River of Grass,* a cultural and natural history of the Everglades that has stayed in print since it was published in 1947. She went on to write other books

about Florida history and botany and hurricanes, as well as novels. But it was *River of Grass* more than anything else, Douglas used to say, that established her direction toward the environmental movement in later years.[4] Although dated, it has become the bible of Everglades protection. In it, her voice was sensitive and intelligent but also unbridled and critical of human arrogance before nature—the same voice heard in her columns and the same voice that served her as an elderly stump speaker and lobbyist trying to save the Everglades.

That voice had evolved during the more than three decades of writing that prepared Douglas for *River of Grass*. After working in the newspaper business, she went on to give nearly two decades to writing short stories. Most are set in contemporary South Florida, and most found an audience in *Saturday Evening Post* readers of the 1920s and 1930s.[5] Two of her stories won O. Henry memorial prizes.[6] It was the heyday of magazine fiction, when popular serials like *Colliers, Saturday Evening Post,* and *Scribner's Magazine* published the top names in the writing business. Douglas sold most of her stories to the *Saturday Evening Post,* which was also a principal venue for F. Scott Fitzgerald.[7]

Much in the way of her contemporaries of letters, such as Eudora Welty and Flannery O'Connor, and the greats who inspired her, particularly Charles Dickens, Douglas wove social criticism into her fiction. Her messages were usually subtle, but her voice was vital. When one compares her newspaper columns of the early 1920s to her short stories, it becomes clear that her literary sensibilities had been molded by the life she had lived and the social concerns to which she had given attention as a journalist. Outrages against humanity are frequent themes in her stories. Many are centered on young people. These are generally underdogs in a struggle against some personal weakness, a doubting or indifferent relative, or some shady figure. Douglas often favored female protagonists. Many reveal autobiographical influences; they are single, intelligent, and determined women with common sense and northern origins.

Gaining a fuller sense of Douglas's own life is key to understanding Douglas the socially conscious writer. She was born on April 7, 1890, in Minneapolis, Minnesota, the only child of Lillian and Frank Stoneman.[8] Her mother was descended from both Cornish and Norman French forebears, a lineage that Douglas found interesting and romantic. Frank

Stoneman grew up in a Quaker colony at Spiceland, east of Indianapolis, and although he valued his Quaker upbringing, he later converted to the Episcopal Church. Frank and Lillian raised their daughter during a time of reform, a circumstance that would later characterize Douglas's journey through life. In the countryside of her native Midwest, farmers were calling for major changes in banking, business, and government. Theirs were the voices that founded the Populist movement, which ascended nearly as rapidly in the national political arena as it plunged. As an adult, Douglas would develop a professional rapport with Mary Bryan, the wife of William Jennings Bryan, the Populist choice for president in 1896.[9]

The America of her youth gave rise to a new crop of reformers, whose impact was more enduring than that of the Populists. They dwelled mostly in the cities and represented numerous social and political interests. Reacting to the problems that came with hasty urbanization and industrialization, they were lumped together under the label of Progressives. In later years, while living in the setting of a young and expanding South Florida city and writing newspaper columns addressing that city's problems, Douglas would herself employ the language of the Progressives.[10]

Her early years, however, were marred by tragedy so severe that it undoubtedly shaped her outlook on life in those later years. When Marjory was three, her father moved the family to Providence, Rhode Island, apparently after his business partnership failed in the Panic of 1893. Success continued to elude Stoneman, and in 1895 his wife, Lillian, suffered a mental breakdown. Mother and daughter left to live under the care of Lillian's family in Taunton, Massachusetts, where Marjory was raised by her grandmother, an aunt, and an uncle. Frank remained in Providence before moving to Florida. The afflicted Lillian meanwhile continued to battle her illness.

Despite the family troubles, young Marjory showed creative talent. In Taunton, she immersed herself in books, probably in part to escape the realities of her life, and began to write. In her high school journal, she noted: "I have always more need of a laugh than a cry, being somewhat disposed to melancholy in my temperament."[11] In 1907, she won a junior writing prize from the *Boston Herald,* which published her story "An Early Morning Paddle." At seventeen, she possessed a keen eye for nature and showed a talent for descriptive writing, as the final passages of her story reveal.

Then a little breeze began to blow which wrinkled the water and began to thin the mist. The east became tinged with pink, which was reflected in the water around him.

Gradually the mist disappeared, the pink streaks became red, then copper-colored and bright gold, until, with a burst of song from the throats of countless birds, the sun itself rose from behind the trees and flooded the pines, the sandy beach, the water and the canoe with a deluge of sunshine.[12]

The next year she published "Waiting for a Train" in the *Taunton High School Journal.* When a freshman in college, she contributed "The Tree Day Pageant at Wellesley" to her old high school journal.[13]

Marjory's college years were invigorating and transforming. She attended Wellesley College and thrived there. Out of "the bewildering presence of boys," she observed in later years, the atmosphere at Wellesley encouraged a student to discover her individual place in the world outside the family. "Despite ourselves, here and there our minds were opened, absorbing beyond our wills, material with which in years to come we might try to answer the eternal question, 'Who am I? What is life?'"[14] Wellesley gave Marjory friends who continued to enrich her life after college. But she valued Wellesley most for what it was: an institution run by women for women, women who wrote books, made scientific discoveries, and blazed trails into male-dominated fields. She had entered college fully expecting to go into teaching, one of the few professions that welcomed her sex. Yet in her junior year, after publishing a story in the *Wellesley Magazine* and being elected to the editorship of the *Senior Annual,* she decided that teaching was not her calling. The announcement of new career intentions met a chilly response back at home. "I remember surprising myself, at a family conference by looking up from a book and saying, 'Really Grandmother, I think I'd rather write.' 'Then you will die in a garret,' my grandmother said."[15]

Marjory graduated from Wellesley with honors in 1912, a year marked also by a crushing blow for her: the death of her mother a few months after her graduation. Marjory felt that her prayers for the restoration of Lillian's health had gone unanswered, and thereupon severed her personal communion with God, eventually losing her religious faith altogether. For the rest of her life, Marjory questioned the very existence of God, and she died a self-proclaimed agnostic.[16]

Tragedy continued to pursue her in those early years. Unable to find

Marjory Stoneman's senior picture at Wellesley College, 1912. Both her formal education and her general experience of life at the women's college awakened her to many of the social and political issues she would later address in The Galley. Courtesy of Florida State Archives.

work as a writer, she took a position as a social worker, as she described it, teaching basic skills to salesgirls at Bamberger's department store in Newark, New Jersey. While living in Newark, she met and married Kenneth Douglas in 1914. He was the religious and social service editor for the local newspaper and was at least thirty years her senior. Within weeks after the honeymoon, Kenneth was arrested for passing a bad check. Marjory waited the six months he spent in the penitentiary, but troubles continued for Kenneth after his release. Marjory's paternal uncle intervened then and persuaded her to leave Kenneth and move to Miami, Florida, to live with her father.[17]

In 1915 Florida was still largely a backwater, a last frontier, as Douglas herself called it. Henry Flagler's recently completed East Coast Railroad, however, was changing the eastern landscape. Terminating in Miami, it was a boon for city boosters, developers, and dreamers. With roughly 11,000

residents and 125,000 annual tourists, Miami was quickly blossoming into a full-fledged city. Its wet environs would within a few years become the swamp salesman's mother lode, and the local population would explode.[18] Frank Stoneman was a key witness of that growth. He had moved to Miami in 1906 and started the city's first morning newspaper.

When his estranged daughter arrived nine years later, Stoneman and his second wife, Lillius, opened their door to her. Marjory quickly learned to appreciate her father's moral integrity, and he would become the most important man in her life. Stoneman the Episcopalian remained true to the humanitarian principles of his Quaker background. "There was always that Quaker touch," Douglas wrote of her father soon after his death in 1941, "the plainness of his speech, his hatred of profanity and gaudy statements, his unpretentiousness, even his grey suits."[19] Stoneman passed his Quaker principles on to his daughter, and they remained a part of her consciousness throughout her life. It was perhaps more than coincidental that Douglas showed a liking for using the word "friends," as in the Quaker tradition, for some of the organizations she later founded or helped found, such as Friends of the University [of Miami] Library, and Friends of the Everglades. "She was the first person to use the word friends in connection with anything in this area," recalled her long-time neighbor and fellow writer Helen Muir.[20] The act of doing so may have been an unconscious one, but Douglas's spiritual link to the Society of Friends was a real and conscious one.

In the Quaker history of social reform, which included figures like Susan B. Anthony and Lucretia Mott, Douglas found a ready model. The Society of Friends, for instance, had been among the most prominent of the religious groups that opposed slavery. Douglas took pride in the fact that her father's parents, Mark Davis and Aletha White Stoneman, left Virginia for Indiana to avoid raising their children in a slaveholding society. The ancestor who stimulated Douglas most as a "free thinker and an activist" was Levi Coffin, reputed president of the Underground Railroad and uncle by marriage of grandmother Stoneman.[21] She frequently acknowledged her famous ancestor and even wrote, but never published, a story about him inspired in part by family lore.[22]

Douglas also appreciated her father's "Quaker sense" about the sexes, meaning he made no distinction between the intellectual capacity of men and women.[23] Upon Douglas's arrival in Miami, there was an immediate

attraction between the minds of father and daughter. Intellectually, Douglas was every bit the equal of her father, who possessed, in her words, a "rich" and "well-stocked" mind.[24] Douglas was a bright, highly literate, and well-informed woman with her own opinions and the ability to articulate them. Recognizing as much, Stoneman put his daughter to work on the newspaper. She served as society-page editor, with occasional opportunities for general-assignment reporting, and when her father took a short leave, she was given temporary charge of the editorial page. She soon learned that life in South Florida offered a degree of stability and predictability that she had not known since college. "It was a great leap forward in my individuality," Douglas later reflected.[25]

Her new job put her in position to move within the centers and among the people of power. In 1916, Mary Bryan recruited her to work for women's suffrage. It was the beginning of a long life of social activism for Douglas. For part of 1917 and 1918, she served as chairperson of the press committee of the Florida Equal Suffrage Association.[26] She also joined a seasoned group of women activists who traveled to Tallahassee to speak before a joint session of the state legislature on behalf of suffrage. Among the lobbyists were Annie Broward, widow of former governor Napoleon Bonaparte Broward, and May Mann Jennings, widow of former governor Frank E. Jennings.[27]

In the midst of the struggle for suffrage rights, America entered the Great War in Europe and Douglas enlisted in the navy. She had hoped to go overseas, but she was disappointed to travel no farther than her yeoman's desk in Miami. After a year she resigned from the navy and signed on for an eighteen-month tour of duty in Europe with the Red Cross. Much like her future fellow Floridian Ernest Hemingway, who witnessed in France the inhumanity of man at war, and later wrote about it, Douglas traveled across the battle-scarred landscape of a crushed and starving continent.[28] The images of Europe never left her, and she occasionally alluded to her experiences in her newspaper column and her short stories of later years, as Hemingway fashioned his into autobiographical fiction. She addressed the horrible waste of human resources during time of conflict and the reduction of the individual to a faceless and expendable unit.[29]

Seasoned by her experiences with war, Douglas returned to the *Herald* in January 1920. At thirty dollars a week, she became an assistant editor, a literary critic, and a columnist. Most of her productivity went into the

daily column that she launched that year and called The Galley Proof, which she later shortened to The Galley. Douglas gave much to her columns and seemed to have fun doing so. Indeed, she proved to be prolific columnist and rarely missed a day. She also displayed an enormous capacity for humor. It undoubtedly stimulated her imagination and helped her cope with sensitive topics and the demand of daily deadlines. Both her professional dedication and sense of humor are evident in a parting passage printed before leaving for her first vacation from The Galley.

> With this coming into port of our weather beaten ship, the Galley, the galley slave wishes to state that in conference with the owners of the ship of sapiency, it has been decided that the galley slave is due for a bit of shore leave. . . . The galley slave, whose oar has often proved merely a reed, cannot speak too highly of those who have allowed this barge of bunkum to range free without sailing order. We assure everyone that our course has been by dead reckoning alone. With these acknowledgments, therefore, the galley slave slips from the rower's bench, leaving the little ship to others who have promised to deal with her gently. Our shore leave is not for long, since we are one of those seafarers to whom the dusty plains are dangerous, unlike the safe watery roadway under our Galley's keel.
>
> But at the same time, while we are delighted to be polite and all that, we're here to tell the horny-handed young stevedores who are going to take on our job that if they think they can run up the black flag and wreck this Galley on any reefs whatsoever, they'll have to keep busy at the pumps. They'll walk the plank in a week if there's any suggestion of mutiny whatsoever.
>
> A-a-a-a-all ashore that's going ashore.[30]

Douglas was different from the average columnist of a local newspaper who always focused on one area of life or limited each column to a single issue. Like the breadth of the wide-brim hats she was famous for in later years, the content of a single column typically covered a range of issues. On occasion, she preceded the column with a poem of her own composition or included a short review of a book she had recently read. Encouraging the poetry and the book reviews, her editors at the *Herald* also expected her to focus on city beautification and improvement. While she did often write about flowers and sunsets and tree planting, she was equally at ease discussing party politics, voting, human welfare, poverty, and civil liberties—all important problems of the day. Both in verse and dialogue, she could be intellectual, humorous, political, antipolitical, and philosophical, from one

day to the next or all in the same column. Just as Douglas the environmentalist berated politicians with vigor, Douglas the columnist never seemed to pull a punch. But she did usually soften the blow by adding a touch of irony.

Reading the columns, one senses a budding writer finding her voice and style and her politics. Her nonfiction prose is as eloquent and as engaging as the fiction that followed in later years. No longer a slave of the society page, as were other newspaper women of her generation, Douglas was breaking into a field of newspaper journalism dominated by men.[31] She was as fully qualified as perhaps any newspaper writer of her day to comment on local, state, national, and international matters. She was well educated and well traveled, and she consumed several newspapers a day and several books a week. She remained ever the scholar, reading widely in literature, poetry, history, and science.

A vibrant and ponderous mind was at work behind each column. On issues of human welfare, particularly when women or children were involved, Douglas's commentary typically took a liberal, or progressive, position. She carried the baton of disfranchised groups, and showed no tolerance for insensitive policymakers. She hated big government but accepted an expanded bureaucracy to serve the needs of the needy. At the same time, waste, incompetence, and corruption in government incensed her. She was no fan of the corporate world and the cozy relationship it often maintained with politicians. Many of the personal values manifested in the Galley were later resurrected in her short stories, and a half a century later the same moral force and candor that characterized her columns drove her message, not only in print but also in speeches, when she campaigned to save the Everglades. The necessary intellectual and value foundation had long been in place when Douglas became an environmental activist.

One can actually trace Douglas's environmental sensibilities late in the century back to the humanitarian concerns conveyed in The Galley. Douglas cared about the endangered environment because she had spent a lifetime caring about people. She recognized the same culture that exploited human beings exploited the Everglades. Yet her views on the environment had not yet fully evolved when she began her work as a columnist. Like most intellectuals, her mind was in a state of constant development. In the 1920s she still accepted the mainstream belief in human control of nature.[32] This is evident in an ode she wrote on the construction of the Tamiami

Trail, the federal highway that bisected the Everglades and disrupted their natural flow, and in her support of the agricultural development of the Everglades (see chapter 2). In later years, she decried both.

Douglas the columnist, however, was anything but insensitive to nature. Quickly upon disembarking from Flagler's train in 1915, she fell in love with the natural environment of South Florida. It was probably her most frequent source of inspiration for column topics, and it remained an important literary backdrop during her short-story years. In the 1920s Douglas had no journalistic equal in Miami when it came to extolling the profusion and beauty of nature in South Florida.

It was in part Douglas's eloquent descriptions of Caribbean pine trees, evening sunsets, and moonlit waters that won The Galley many fans. George Merrick, Coral Gables' highly influential developer, said that every morning he turned to Douglas's column with "lively anticipation." A local attorney praised Douglas's "philosophic deductions," but he was particularly taken with her writing, which he ranked "with the very best from any pen." Her poetry was especially popular. It was good enough for reprinting in other newspapers and acceptance by *Scribner's* magazine.[33] In a letter addressed to "MSD," Douglas's column signature, one reader described her as a gift from the "fair Aphrodite," bestowed with poetic words of "honey and velvet and gold."[34]

Douglas sought not simply to please her readers. She wanted to make them think, and she often employed her words as an instrument of social change. She suspected that her voice, conveyed through pen and typewriter, was more potent than her vote. In her diary she quoted a passage from the nineteenth-century writer and social critic Henry George that framed her belief: "Social reform is not to be secured by noise and shouting, by complaints and denunciations, by the formation of parties or the making of revolutions but by the awakening of thought and the progress of ideas."[35]

As a voice in what became South Florida's most important newspaper, Douglas helped awaken a budding metropolis to many ideas and issues. Much was astir in domestic and world events for which she offered comment and verse. When she began her column, the United States was fresh out of the war in Europe; the League of Nations was newly formed to preserve world peace; Congress had failed to ratify the Versailles Treaty to end the war officially; and the Bolsheviks in Russia had been in power for three years. On the domestic side, the country was in the midst of a presidential

election that included the Republican Warren Harding, the Democrat James Cox, and the socialist Eugene V. Debs; women would vote for the first time in a national election; prohibition was in full force; moral stewards, along with the U.S. attorney general and the U.S. postmaster, were repressing freedom of expression; silent films were emerging as a favorite pastime; and Ernest Hemingway and F. Scott Fitzgerald were at the literary forefront. Locally, Miami was experiencing the pains of a booming city. Real estate was the hottest commodity and offered some of the hottest newspaper topics around. Developers were clearing land and filling swamps for commercial and residential construction.[36]

During her three years with The Galley, as a result of these developments, Douglas created a valuable repository of social and political commentary and history. When she wrote her last column, for the July 31, 1923, issue, she was seeking to join the literary world of Hemingway and Fitzgerald. The strain of meeting a daily deadline had taken its toll, but she also felt the need for more creative control in her work. Left behind at the *Herald* and folded between the pages of back issues was the work of a woman who would become one of the most important figures in twentieth-century Florida and one of its most insightful observers.

Until now, that work has been left untapped. The volume in hand offers a sampling of Douglas's musing and poetry from the more than one thousand columns she produced. Those reprinted here were chosen for their historical significance, poignancy, wittiness, and provocativeness. Braiding commentary with relevant verse, much as Douglas did in The Galley, I have arranged the selections chronologically in chapters that reflect the many voices of Douglas: that of nature lover, South Florida booster, political analyst, social progressive, intellectual, philosopher—and often, simply, just that of a woman. Her ideas for column material came from conversations with colleagues and friends, the countless newspapers and books she read, daily observations she logged in a notebook (which in the column she called "From the Day Book of a Journalist"), and her nimble imagination. Revisiting Douglas's early writings will heighten the reader's sense of her broad intelligence, writing talent, and insight. Her columns give the reader of today early-twentieth-century eyes for the way of things not just in 1920s Miami or Florida but also in America generally. A half century before Marjory Stoneman Douglas was the "voice of the river," she was the voice of daily life.

Prologue

When Douglas launched The Galley on March 7, 1920, she could not be sure where the venture would take her or how it would impact her life as a writer. She wanted to maintain creative control of the column's content, but she was realistic about having to answer to editors, which included her father. The Galley was the most diverse and creative column in the *Herald* of her day, however, and her imagination seems to have overridden editorial interference. She, in fact, enjoyed having fun in her column playing up the idea of a power struggle between editor and writer. The opening passage of her inaugural column, quoted below, set the tone for the voice of the Galley Slave, as she liked to call herself. Although she questioned whether she was embarking on a happy venture, her words suggest to the reader that enjoyment, and even a bit of zaniness, lay ahead. A year later, when she outlined her reason for choosing to call her column The Galley, she again indicated that humor, playfulness, and creativity were her priorities. Even as she devoted discussion to subjects of a serious nature, she planned to have fun with her daily assignment.

❧❧

We have spent two days and parts of two nights, when the neighbor's baby and dog howled and woke us up, thinking up a good snappy lead for this here colyum. And we have come to the conclusion that the columnists BLT and FPA and Don Marquis are right. A colyum conductor's life is not a happy one. But we said we would do a colyum and do a colyum we will, even if the Original Editor [her father, Frank Stoneman] cans all our brightest and pet ideas. We hasten to add, to all readers of the South's Only Newspaper [the *Miami Herald*] who wish to see in print any little gem of

thought, prose, poetry or anything, which their wife or second cousin think is funny, that the Proof Reader will award to the Day's Brightest not only the top of the galley but the added incentive of the Brown Derby, the Fur Lined Bathtub and the Barbed Wire Ear Muffs.

(March 7, 1920)

And speaking of The Galley, which we do occasionally, we have been asked why we call it that and what the point is, anyway. Well, of course, in the first place, there isn't too much point. It is a great mistake to have a too much pointed title. Suppose you call it "Jokes and Worse," why, you might not be able to live up to it. And if you called it "The Top o' the Morning," it wouldn't be true, because we generally get down to work about half past nine. And so back in the dark ages when we thought of such a thing we called it The Galley, for the simple reason that the distinguished editor of the South's Only [the *Miami Herald*] wouldn't let us call it the Hell Box, which is what we wanted. "The Hell Box" would be really a nice one, you see, because it is the box where all the dead type goes, all the odds and ends that aren't wanted by any one else out in the composing room. Now a galley is a long strip of some metallic substance which will hold just a column of type, so that it can be handled easily. And as our column is, of course, the most important thing out there we call it The Galley to distinguish it from all the others. It's a nice, handy sort of name, and it doesn't mean anything we can't live up to, and then you can make puns about it and a Roman boat and a galley slave, as well as the place on a ship where the ship's cook cooks up all kinds of messes and for various other reasons. That's why we call it The Galley, but you'd better cut this bit out and put it in your pocketbook or you won't remember it all when some one asks you. It's a bit like "the better 'ole." If we could find one, we'd crawl into it.

(June 7, 1921)

∽ 1 ∽ Nature Lover

Douglas was never more creative and descriptive than when she was writing about birds and trees and powerful weather and sunsets. The selections in this chapter offer some of her earliest writings on nature.

When she wrote her columns in the 1920s, she was not yet the consummate environmentalist that she would become in later years. She recognized the uniqueness of the Everglades, for instance, but she had not come to realize their biological importance. Few people had. Although she wrote sympathetically about fauna of South Florida, she reduced nature's creatures to categories of good and bad, as is evident by the first entry below in which she describes and celebrates the killing of a water moccasin. She was, nevertheless, slowly being drawn toward a greater environmental awareness, in part because as a keen observer of nature, she had always been captured by its beauty and its sheer impact upon the senses.

One of her earliest revealed traits as a child, in fact, had been a sympathy for natural things. In her autobiography, she recalls having cried when her father read a passage from *Hiawatha* in which a birch tree sacrifices its bark for the building of a canoe. From her very first publication at the age of seventeen, a short story that appeared in the *Boston Herald* in 1907, the natural landscape provided the primary colors on her writer's palette. She was taken with such nature writers as W. H. Hudson, of whom she would write a biography.[1] When she moved south, the unique environment of South Florida would both fascinate and inspire her more than any other place or thing. This was especially true of the white light of the tropical sun. Throughout her life, she was enamored of the sun's warmth, its brightness, and its seldom-obscured presence in the South Florida sky. She would go on to describe it in many ways, but almost always as white, in all the genres in which she wrote—newspaper copy, short stories, books, and verse.

Douglas had only to look to her immediate surroundings to find the subjects on which as a columnist and budding writer she could practice her prose.

But she wrote about nature's beauty not simply because she was inspired by it. She wanted to convey to her readers an appreciation of South Florida's natural wonders. The descriptive prose in her columns reflected an environmental ethic that valued the existence of the nonhuman world. Douglas equated an eye for natural beauty with "spiritual common-sense," and she preached that humans could learn something from observing nature, that indeed wisdom came from knowing and being one with the earth. Ultimately, she wanted others to know what she observed every day—that South Florida, beyond its people and human history, was special because of its sky, land, and water, and all the things that trimmed the landscape with the color and activity of life. On countless occasions, therefore, her words brought the natural world of South Florida to life within the prosaic confines of the two-inch-wide newspaper column.[2]

The Confessions of the Galley Slave.

Every Saturday afternoon there comes a moment, about 3 o'clock, when the Slave of the Galley realizes that everything is easy to resist but temptation. For at that time, with the Galley for Sunday on the book in the composing room and the rest of the chores out of the way comes the moment to decide. Last Saturday the question was, "Shall we finish the Galley for Monday now and have Sunday morning off, or shall we work Sunday morning and go fishing now?"

And as this is being written on Sunday morning and we are conscious of more freckles the inference is easy. We went fishing.

Out on the road that runs, straight as a die from horizon to horizon between the levels of the Everglades; the world on a hot Saturday afternoon is a brilliant and glittering place. The sky is hot white, the road is white and from the grass and palmettos of the dried sloughs a thousand tiny points of light glitter in the sun. The canal water is a clear brown, rippling and sparkling in the good wind and overhead a buzzard or two, ragged wing tips silhouetted like Japanese ink against the glare, swing and wheel.

With her cat on the front steps of her house in Coconut Grove, 1920s. Douglas used to say that observing her cats helped her to identify with creatures in the wild. Courtesy of Florida State Archives.

When at last you reach the right spot the car is drawn up, the new leaders tied on the line and the salt pork solemnly cut. Breathlessly, you watch the first cast, the swing of the wrist, the little ripple where the bait drops, the tiny flash of white as it is drawn below the surface. Then the business of fishing really commences.

Out here in the 'glades it is still as still. The cool winds rustle the palmettos a little. A fish jumping downstream hits the water again with a flat tail. A horse fly or two circles around your head, droning sleepily.

Then somebody gets a bite. A jerk upward and the line swings high, with a flash of frantic silver flapping at its end. We run up to see the luck. Oh, wonderful sign, it is a bass, if a tiny one. We all determine to catch nothing but bass for the rest of the afternoon.

But the garfish bite and steal bait, the little bream nibble daintily and we pull them out, openly apologetic but inwardly elated at catching anything. And every once in a while someone really gets a bass, nearly a foot long, a fat and gray beauty to add to the lengthening string tied to a stick and cooling at the water's edge.

All the while the colors in the perfect arch of the sky are growing clearer as the shadows lengthen. First they are faint turquoise, then a deeper blue, with great white cloud masses that lift up and up into the dazzle. And then the sun, a perfect round of molten rose, pushes below the cloud bank westward and it is almost sunset.

For a while there is fishing. The little gnats are out and the surface of the waters is alive with the concentric circles of moving arrow heads of the striking fish. But it is fast work, for the dusk comes suddenly, the car must be turned around and the roughest stretch of roadway covered in the first dark.

But just as the last fish is put on the string the climax of the day occurs. Across the water, straight for us, comes the wedge shaped and looping slim length of a water moccasin. War is declared, as he hits the bank, and although he struggles for cover around a boulder, death is swift and inevitable under the jagged rocks that are hurled at his evil length. Triumphantly he is fished out and stretched on the roadway before being flung back again to the all-devouring gars.

With the great levels of the 'glades flowing darkly by on either side of the white road, with the stars out and the moon high and the wind sweet and cool, we decide that a really successful fishing trip, with a moccasin hunt added, is worth working Sunday morning, and more. And besides. The bass are delicious broiled.

(April 26, 1920)

Tropic Summer.
Northward the spring still paints the hills
 Timid delights and April ways.
Summer in Florida now sets
 Ablaze its dawns and burnished days.

White hot the curtain of the sky,
 Crimson the poinciana lifts
And all our tropic ecstacy,
 marks where the summer heaps its gifts.

Purple the splendid spread of sea
 Creams on the sands its sunny tides

Fountains of green, the palm trees swing
 Full in the wind the white gull rides.

Sunsets that burn in unguessed fire,
 Dusk blue and swift as heron's wing
Then from the darkening sea the stars,
 Then from the east the nights that sing.

Oh velvet glory of the dark.
 Oh living bosom of that sea.
Regal the nights whose splendor sets
 Oh summer her full majesty.

(April 27, 1920; reprinted in the Southern Review, *June 1920)*

A Plea for Wider Justice.

The little wiggly single worm
When trodden on ungently
Can be depended on to turn
(A poor rhyme, incidently)
But what I mean is just that he
Is similar to you and me.

An oyster, bivalve, placid, calm,
Will get quite vexed by grit,
Protecting its fat self from harm
By coating over it.
It makes a pearl of white smooth beauty
Nor ever prates of "art" or "duty."

The jelly fish when prodded shrinks
As you and I do.
Thus proving that who thinks he thinks
May know a thing or two.
But this I state, for his correction.
He always acts for his protection.

So let's extend democracy
To fit these things inferior,

Who really aren't, because you see
We're not darned superior.
We only like to think we are.
But they aren't so particular.

(January 3, 1921)

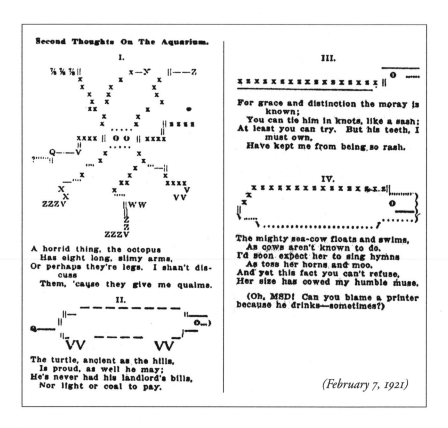

Second Thoughts On The Aquarium.

I.

A horrid thing, the octopus
Has eight long, slimy arms,
Or perhaps they're legs. I shan't discuss
Them, 'cause they give me qualms.

II.

The turtle, ancient as the hills,
Is proud, as well he may;
He's never had his landlord's bills,
Nor light or coal to pay.

III.

For grace and distinction the moray is
 known;
 You can tie him in knots, like a sash;
At least you can try. But his teeth, I
 must own,
 Have kept me from being so rash.

IV.

The mighty sea-cow floats and swims,
 As cows aren't known to do.
I'd soon expect her to sing hymns
 As toss her horns and moo,
And yet this fact you can't refuse,
Her size has cowed my humble muse.

(Oh, MSD! Can you blame a printer
because he drinks—sometimes?)

(February 7, 1921)

There is a certain wisdom shared chiefly by farmers and naturalists and
shrewd old women who have borne many children. It is a wisdom some-
how related to the earth from which wisdom comes. It is a wisdom which
few politicians, and no active politicians, and not very many city dwellers,
can share. It is related to the slow growths of things, the sure succession of
the seasons and the infinite patience and the infinite labor of natural pro-
cesses. They know that there is a great deal of sound and fury in the world,
and that there has been a good deal of sound and fury, and, in all probabil-

ity, there will continue to be. They know that the nature of trees is one thing and that the nature of plants is one thing and the nature of babies one thing, and the nature of man, one thing. And they know that to be near the earth and thinking the thoughts of the earth, finding out what they are, by learning what it is, is a great honor and a great necessity. That is why farmers are generally quiet men, not joining eagerly into the hurly-burly of trumpery discussion, why naturalists are safe men, not being too ready with creeds and formulas, why old women who have borne many children are shrewd women, having learned the terrible implacability of nature and the ruthless desire for liberation that is life itself. To such there is no wisdom that is not related to the earth, or does not partake of its nature. And it is this to which America, having completed its work of hasty development is now turning.

(December 8, 1921)

Look out your window. Can you see a pine tree? If you can, you're lucky. They are going fast. And every day somebody cuts down a few more to make a new subdivision that, without them, will be as raw and ugly as plain dirt without trees can be. Do you own a pine tree? Then you are lucky. But if you appreciate it, you are more than that. You have a genuine eye for beauty, which is another word for spiritual common-sense.

(December 20, 1921)

Before the Storm.

Late in the green and brooding end of day,
The wind dropped breathless and the leaves were still;
Only a sliding ripple from the bay
Brimmed the slow river to its gleaming fill.
Clouds bloomed at sunset flame and daffodil,
Softer than dreaming in the western way,
'Til the day blossomed from the sea, until
Night in dead black and mute, expectant lay.
The dark waits murky and the moss is bowed,
Our footsteps muffle as the hot dew drips,

Stars overhead stand faint in misted shroud.
Moment by moment falters and time slips
As words move slowly from our sluggish lips.

(October 17, 1922)

Black Moonlight.

What god, what small, mad, understanding god,
Dreamed this sharp moonlight and the black wet leaves,
Where drips and quiet drips the rainy eaves
When moon, stripped naked, stares upon the sod?

So where the path burns, white and whiter white,
Cut by hard patterns of the orange trees,
One brittle glitter, waits upon no breeze,
Stabbing this moment on the brilliant night.

Holding, in diamond and cleaving line
This moment, acid. All eternity
May be this moment, though not you or I
Yet, Shall entrap it with yours, or mine.

(October 7, 1922)

The Resourceful Mrs. Nature.

A red-headed woodpecker on our sill
Gives a fratt-tatt-tatt as he works his will,
And I very much wonder, as his bill strikes deep,
If he'll leave us a roof and a place to sleep,
But the spiders' webs on the live oak tree
Are a joy and a marvel, and a jewel to see.
So perhaps when the woodpecker's ruined our roof
We can tent ourselves with the spider's woof.

(November 10, 1922)

The Japanese symbol for happiness is the pine tree.

(November 11, 1922)

River Water.

Out in the islets of the ghostly night
 Where the wind in a murmuring moonlight flows,
I hear the sound of the river water
 Leaping the bank where the new grass grows.

All night long underneath the rustles
 Of tree to a bird or drip from the eaves
I'm listening still to the river water,
 Cool as the littlest sound of leaves.

Black, with a star that is just a glimmer
 Or rippled with gilt in the dawn and grey,
Still comes the sound of the river water
 Voices that whisper the sea to stay.

So have they murmured since land was lifted
 Out of the glamorous deeps of sea;
The shimmering deeps that the river water,
 Listens for, quivers for, longs to be.

(November 12, 1922)

From the Day Book of a Journalist.

Thursday, 9 November.

Fourteen fat brown and white ducks waddling in a drove, or a covey, or a flock, or whatever ducks do waddle in, quacking like a pastoral symphony on brilliant green grass, under live oak trees, with a puddle flashing back the sky in the white road and leading the ducks on, that is one of the jolliest things I know. I never realized before what a lot a string of ducks add to a landscape. But there is something so domestic and familiar about them, perhaps because of all the goose girls in the fairy tales, or the background of tradition we have left over from countries where ducks and geese and sheep are in the common speech as they are in our Mother Goose rhymes. I cannot resist watching them as they come quacking across the road, all pushing and shoving busily, because some duck ahead has found a patch of good weed. Whenever their cackling rises a little higher I always have to dash to

the window, to watch an automobile pushing its way slowly among them, or a child playing with them. But best, I like the way they push their broad breasts into the duck pond that the rains have made, and oar away serenely, changing their quacking voices to the reedy, throaty call that is the most watery sound I know. And then the fun of seeing them stand on their heads and skitter their tails. Really, a herd or a school or a covey or a swarm, or whatever you call it, of ducks, should be included with every pastoral vista. A sunny afternoon is not complete without them.

(November 13, 1922)

Honey of the Morning.

Now is the time fallen on such mellowness
That all the skies are honey of tenderness;
Days are but droning bees humming in yellowness
Over the flower of sea, blue in the sun.

Wise are the gulls rising in sun and soaring
Drunk with the day, flashing with white wing oaring,
Beautiful, whizzing by in the white light pouring
Beauty and earth and the gulls tremendously one.

Lift the cup of this world eagerly;
Feel all your body braced on the earth vividly;
Drink with your heart and your body these days greedily,
Time is a stream and a silence soon to be won.

(November 20, 1922)

From the Day Book of a Journalist.

Friday, 17 November.

A soft, grey green, infinitely soothing day, yet a day so different from the smoky greys of the north that there is no comparison. No matter how deep the clouds are the clearness of the light still penetrates, much as the light penetrates softly the green levels of the sea. In such sunlessness the grass is vivid green, jade, emerald, the greenest thing in the world, and you can see,

in the backgrounds of lush foliage almost hundreds of other shades and tints of green, the dark blue green of hibiscus leaves or shiny dark blue green of orange and grapefruit leaves, the pale yellow tip leaves against the darker leaves of the mastic, the silver of the live oaks, the black-green of loquats, the pink tips of new mango leaves and all the delicate difference of tone and shadow and lighting which on bright days half shut your eyes. Those soft grey days are really exquisite; with a soft wind booming in from the sea and the birds rioting and calling and twittering out of sight somewhere in the intervals of showers.

(November 21, 1922)

It was our privilege a little before twilight an afternoon recently, to be taken to see one of the oldest places in Coconut Grove which has never been manicured by a landscape gardener or cleared from its original planting since the first, but which has quietly gone on growing during the drums and tramplings of a thousand real estate men beyond its gates, a bit of old South Florida, as lovely, as remote, as anything in the South Sea isles. You enter by a gate which is just another of those gates along that mellow Coconut Grove road. Beyond that the path winds and twists slowly, plunging you almost at once in a jungle growth which almost meets over your head. Huge Caribbean pine trees dispute the way of the jungle at first, but their place is taken by enormous gumbo limbo, by live oaks, by a dark feathery jacaranda and countless other shrubs and trees and creepers, making a green gloom of the fading light. Your footsteps are silent on dark soft earth and you go softly, too, hushed. The clearing opens beyond the path end with a wide lawn of rank soft grass which has not been cut, but allowed to grow free right to the steps of the house, a huge dark brown shape in the gathering twilight, reticent, moody perhaps, but utterly in keeping with its surroundings. Far down the slope that leads to the far glimpses of the bay there are other great Caribbean pines, enormous, mysterious, the true pine of South Florida, hoary as if with forgotten survivals from the sea. Down the grassy slope the path slips silently through air brown with the luminousness of twilight, down to the levels of palms and black shaggy masses of bamboo. But you hardly notice those at first, for straight beyond, as lofty, as permanent, as granite, as stone pillars move two rows of royal palms, reaching in utter majesty out to the afterglow of sunset, fit altar for

their tremendous cathedral. Through all this there is not the slightest
sound. You stand gazing, in silence, wholly in reverence. It is a cathedral
which needs no incense nor requires worshipers. But when you turn, the
sunset is a blaze of flat gold behind the huge pines on the hill and you know
that this dimness, this immense green, is the very secret place of old South
Florida, for which there were never any Druids, elemental, mysterious,
hoary, but young with the youth of all the world, of all growth, of all life. It
is a very wonderful thing to have been allowed to tiptoe over its threshold.

(December 3, 1922)

 Pine Land.

 Far off, the pine, like lovely smoke,
 March windily against the sky.
 And never poplar, spruce nor oak
 Was rarer to my heart, say I.

 Who stands to gaze a-sunsetward
 And loves that laced, enchanted line
 Feels close around him beauty's guards,
 Strong and serene as rampart pine.

 (December 20, 1922)

The porpoise are coming into the bay again occasionally and it is earnestly
hoped that no fisherman ever kills one. I can't imagine why they would, but
then some people would kill anything. The porpoise are such jolly little
fellows and they go dipping and rolling out in the turquoise water so very
effectively that it would be nice if there were a lot more. According to
"Moby Dick" a porpoise is a near relative of a whale but at any rate their
black sleekness is quite an event in the bay.

And have you noticed how many sea gulls there seem to be, more now
than ever. I don't exactly know how to go about encouraging the sea gull to
settle here, but they surely ought to be encouraged. Of course they have a
practical value as scavengers but they are such beautiful things anyway, their
flight is so white and sweeping and free and lovely and they are so much the

spirit of the sea ways, with their eery crying into the wind and their clean whizzing flight about the tall masts of ships and the docks and the water front and the stretches of open water. Is it San Francisco or Seattle or where that they have a monument to the sea gulls, a straight white shaft surmounted by three or four gulls in stone at the very end of a long jetty.

That sort of intimate monument is so much greater addition to a city than one of those cold and proper affairs of some prominent and highly uninteresting gentleman wrapped up in a marble frock coat.

(January 30, 1923)

The sunset Thursday night was one of those things which it is worth coming to South Florida to see and to remember. It must have been perfectly amazing across the bay, those great swathes and streaks of rose color sky. But I saw it from behind the dark live oak trees in Spring Garden and it was something before which to be awed. There it seemed to burn with those metallic and intense colors which molten brass gives forth, glowing and sultry, radiating a sense of fire, if no fire itself, stamped against the background of sky which was steel blue and apple green beyond the cloud flecks. Behind the bars of the last fringe of pine, and behind the dark moss hanging off the oaks, with each tiny leaf cut into black velvet silhouette against that burning, the sunset blazed its silent conflagration and the river, a gleam silently curving, smoldered beneath that sky, red and more red as if the very earth was transparent. So the moment of sunset hung silent, airy heat, immense and metallic and blazing. Then it ceased to be, and the swift twilight drawing grey veils hurriedly for the night's pageant, when the fire was forgotten and the moon slid slowly in dripping pearl, over pearly sea.

(February 5, 1923)

There are times when one has to change one's mind a little bit about Australian pines. Of course, one is tired of them and of their constant use, to the exclusion of other and lovelier trees. But when one wakes up with the infinite sighing of the Australian pines in one's ears as if it were a deep tide running crystal overhead, and when one catches a glimpse of their high tops flowing with the wind in that veiled and harmonious way they have one's heart melt to them. In their place and when they are very tall and have

fitted into their landscape, they give an undoubted quality to the whole
atmosphere of this country.

(February 6, 1923)

Down the Keys.

There is left nothing here but vastness
And underneath an abiding simplicity.
High overhead the sky leaps upward.
The keys are low mounds of mangrove.
A little wind rises and runs murmuring
Where the sun makes soft jade of the outer reaches of the sea.

Down in the shadow of the boat the water chuckles.
The water is clear and brown around the water weeds
A heron steps carefully out from the mangrove roots.
He is the same color as the roots.
We are shadow drifting past him in the sunshine.
With the heron we savor the silence.

Like dim whales the distant keys lie in the morning.
Far away there is a white boat.
Nothing is so clean as this water
Unless it is the wind.
Are you thinking of anything?
There is nothing to think of
Only of sun and wind
And the quiet talking of the water about the bow.

A thousand years of this would heal cities.
Ten years of this would make whole any mutilation.
A day of this makes silence blossom in your heart.
When the light changes this sea will be sapphire.
The shadows of mangroves in water will be purple.
There will be rose-gold in the sky
And perhaps star light.
What do they mean by pavements and offices?

The fish drift brown shadows in brown shadows.
The ripples gleam in the brown water, the living water.
Hush, let us not make any noises.
Hardly any motion, hardly any thinking.

There is a little sound of leaves in stillness.
A curved leaf drops to the water with a small sound.
It is enough to be hushed in this stillness.
It is enough to know silence with one's whole body.
There is nothing here but vastness and simplicity.
It will be something to remember,
 some day, on a street corner.

(February 7, 1923)

The Color of Sea-Water.

Drowned in white radiance from the utter pinnacles of sky,
This sea burns
Jewel—
Fire—
Crucible of unspeakable beauty,
Burning and molding sea-beauty deep in the fibre of man.

Blue—
Blue beyond all imagining—
Lapis and sapphire hollows
Swelling and bursting to crests of unimaginable dazzle,
Deeper than the forgotten meanings of things,
Deep as the intimate foundations of worlds.
Burn, blue of sea water,
Shaken and mutable thunder
Burn, blue,
Scorch, sear.
Let him come clean from your fires who can endure you.
Let him be branded with the brand of your splendor
 forevermore.

Green—
Molten, fluid
Liquid and unbelievable jade,
Burn, green,
Blazing your luminous emeralds in broad bands of quivering
 light,
Streaked and banded and blazing,
Bursting and foaming,
Bursting in trembling fire and quicksilver clean to the edge of
 the world.
How shall any man live unmoved in the heart of your
 radiance?
How shall he stand without staggering?
How shall he live unmarked with the mark of your terror
 forevermore?
Who have endured your beauty, O sea,
Who have sustained you,
Who have endured,
Who have been burned in the crucible of your burning,
Sea-fire of beauty,
Let them be blinded
Rather than go unquickened hereafter,
Careless among the dusty ways of the world.

(March 27, 1923)

Before 10 o'clock, these days of late tropic spring, the day is like a mirror in which the clouds, the trees, the river and all the thousand spears of the grass rest quiet, waiting. Not a breath mars the smooth brown glass of the river, where the sun gleams, and the leaves on the live oaks and the fronds of the great palms are motionless. Only the birds are unaffected by it, and go shouting and throbbing and thrilling on their own spring affairs. This morning I saw one cardinal, his spring feathers sharp rose against an ineffable sky, at the very top a live oak where the dew still hung, uttering the exquisite song of the cardinal above the singing of all the rest. But suddenly a stir moved on the surface of the river, a stir caught among the leaves,

moved on the grass. A new liveness came into the air, a liveness and an expectancy. And then the wind came, the great tropic wind which waits until the middle of the morning always before riding in from the outer rim of the sea, shattering the mirror of calm and filling the sky and the earth with the big, fresh joyousness of its presence. The coming of the trade wind, in the morning, is one of those experiences which the people who go away early miss, as they miss all the great bloom of tropic spring and summer, upon which, like a new adventure, we are now launched.

(April 17, 1923)

It was very dark, the other night crossing the causeway, one of those windless nights when even the stars are faint and far away and the water stretches for vast miles, inky and slow heaving, freighted with glamor, touched only by the straight, down stabbing daggers of the causeway lights, yellow exclamation points. Now with the glariest lights of the city muted a bit, both shores are a remote lacework of pricked lights and gleams and glints, with here a tall building picked out against the blackness and there, or nearer, only a low red light and a low green light to show where a white yacht silently waits for the sun. The causeway is a bridge of light between blackness and the cars that whine across it are restless souls, going from some unknown heaven or hell and carrying their own lights swinging in their hands. If the cars were stopped there would be only a little sound of wind walking a long way off, and the lipping of the nearest waves against the stones.

(April 18, 1923)

By the way, what has become of all the land crabs. Or at least, it seems to me that I haven't seen any all winter, either struggling on the road or scuttling into their holes by the riverbank or rattling on the cement walks with the tips of their finger nails. Is it that people actually have exterminated them? Or what? Or is it just that the open season for land crabs hasn't yet arrived.

(April 20, 1923)

If I Should Build a House for Me.

If I should build a house to be
A roof between the rain and me,
I'd want it still and grey and wide
For all outdoors to get inside.
I'd want its floor to hold the cool,
Dark, shining look of hidden pool
That mountains know and edge with green
Dim, fern for oreades to screen.

I'd want its walls to be hung round
With skies free curving, endless bound,
One wall for sunsets, one for noons,
And one left very wide for moons.

I'd want the chimney place made high
For flames of all brush fires to fly
And sparks of blazing driftwood glow
As dark sea beaches often know.

I'd want the presence of good trees
Tall groined for ceilings or for frieze
And garden colors, here and there,
On cushions or a friendly chair.

The patio, in living green,
Would be the threshold in between
Where house and earth would quite forget
Which one was which, or where they met.
If I should build a house to be
A roof between the rain and me
I'd want it still and grey and wide
For sun and stars to come inside.

That was rather a startling thing that Dr. Gifford said at the tree planting at the Buena Vista school the other day. He said that in the north we have only about fifty trees to choose from when we plant. Here, we have over five hundred.

(April 21, 1923)

For a New Earth.

Set me this seal upon your heart,
 Stripped by the crystal of these skies,
That from this very earth shall start
 Your promised towers of Paradise.
For who beneath this sun has known
 The ecstacy of white, bright fire,
What other dark shall call his own,
 Where else, the city of his desire?

How shall you drink the deep delight
 Of sea's one gem, of sands long gleam
And fall to lift, far-shining, white,
 The sure foundation of your dream?

That dream, as old as death or birth
 That dream, as new as breath shall be,
A holy city raised from earth,
 Fit for this gorgeous soil and sea.

(April 27, 1923)

People who do not know what acalyphas are have only to look around them. The raw beefsteak shrub, of which they see so much everywhere and which they see more than everything else, is it. The more you see it, the less you like it.

(June 9, 1923)

After Rain.

See what new brilliance after rain,
 When new sun marks morning clouds with gold,
And the small leaves, the grass blades that have lain
Long in the wet, in glitter now unfold.

High frothing in the footsteps of the cloud,
The new winds leap, a great and glorious tide,
Their murmur in the trees grows clear and loud.
In their deep flood the gleaming seagulls ride.

Now the fresh green is mounting in the world,
And after rain, the splendid trees look up,
Now through the city the clean air is hurried,
Brimming with crystal streets like a tall cup.

Oh, that the wind might wash the dim mist far,
Far from these streets that still they fill and choke,
Mists that shut eyes, blind fogs and dull, that mar
The city that should be splendid as that oak.

(June 10, 1923)

Show me an old man planting fruit trees and I'll show you grandchildren that will inherit money.

(June 15, 1923)

Fulfillment.

Spite of beauty, there is pain.
 Spite of sorrow, loveliness.
Men shall find new hope again
 In a green star's loneliness.

Men shall learn their common worth
 Where racked bodies turn to die.
After sunset's dream, is earth.
 After weary earth, the sky.

(June 18, 1923)

There is really nothing more invigorating and thrilling than to ride far out into the Everglades, or into the edge of them, and watch the clouds piling high in great soft toned mountains, over the wide expanse of lavish green earth which opens out on every hand clear to the sharp cut rim of the horizon. With all these rains the greens of tall grass and of crop-land are brilliant, jewel-like. There are thousands of small, half hidden flowers, purple and soft blue and mustard yellow, woven in with the green and under the

driving wind the clouds leave great cracks and clefts for the full dazzle of the sunlight to cut through in great rays and streaks, leaving even more brilliant patches of sun moving across the vast surface of the green. All the little insects are loud in the grass in the sunshine, or, if you are there toward the end of afternoon when the sunset which will presently blazon not just the west with burning, molten gold, but the clouds with white and rosy light; and the east with the pink, is generally imminent, the air will be filled with the quick, circling flight of the whippoorwills, or bull-bats, lifting on sharp, white barred wings to different air levels and supplying the whole of the sky with silent motion. It is quiet out there, except for these small sounds of insects or rustling grass, that it seems that if one could be still enough, and long enough, that same tremendous meaning that is behind this silence would be made known. Or the purpose of the tremendous winds which move and start and come forward or change direction and go roaring away to some other horizon, as if they were the presence of some great being, playful and unwatched here on their vast hearthstone.

(June 23, 1923)

We have been asked from time to time to reprint poems. We have even been asked to get out a book of verse, and we have even thought of it seriously a number of times. But between the difficulty of going over them and picking them out and the difficulty of getting a publisher to believe that our stuff is wanted in book form around here, without much tangible proof we seem not to have gone very far. Now we are wondering what poems people would like to have us put in a book, if we had a book to put them in. Which would you choose? As a beginning, we are reprinting here a whole column of tree poems taken as we found them in our files.

 The Royal Poinciana.
 (In Ceylon the poinciana is thought to be that
 burning bush that appeared to Moses.)

 On a grey tree,
 Late in the spring,
 There comes a miracle—
 Remembering—

Once in a far land
 One passing by
Stopped to see flames leap
 From branches dry.

Moses his name was
 And in that hush
Angel of Heaven spoke
 Out of the bush.

So when the spring comes,
 Out of dark sod,
Burns here that grey tree,
 Gorgeous with God.

I am the Mangrove.

 I am the mangrove
 I build.
Quietly, quietly, through the blazing days,
Through the breathing nights I thrust my grey roots,
 Building.

 Under the great sky
 My leaves are lavish.
But down in the dark water, the quiet water,
The brown water, my roots arch, moving
 Steadfastly.

 The winds move
 But I move not.
I buttress myself with toughness,
I reach my roots down into the roots of things,
 Foundations.

 The waters move,
 But I move not.
Day by day the shining brown ripples stir in my shadows.
Night by night the dark tides tug and lift at my arches
 Impotently.

Silently, silently,
Out of sea refuse,
Out of the brown seaweed, the beach grass, the mud,
Out of the flotsam and jetsam of the winds and the waters,

I build.
I build
Striding.
Behind me grows a barrier, woven of my roots;
Behind me advances the armies of the conquering grass,
Dry footed.

I shout my challenge,
Silently, silently,
I stride, triumphant.
Buffeted, victorious, out across shallows, out to the sea ways,
I am the pioneer, I am the forerunner,
I am the adventurer.
After me comes earth.
I am the mangrove.
Look.
I build.

Sunsets Through the Cutler Pines.
Late in the day when the sun is low,
And the wind is fresh from the distant sea,
Down through the pines it is good to go,
And be one with all earth ways silently.

Fingers of sun slant in tawny gold;
Creeping and feeling the shadows crawl,
The wind is sweet with the pine sweet mold,
And the turquoise of the sky is over all.

Still as a tree and still as the sky,
Stand and hold open your heart like a cup,
And the balm of the earth with brim with a sigh,
And the savor of the sea will lift you up.

Stand and renew all the peace in your heart,
 Stand and feel through you the Stillness grow.
Earth sweet and savor's the wisest path,
 And the way of the tree is the way to go.

To a Pine Tree.

If you were set in Samarcand,
 Behind the seven seas,
Unheeded so you would not stand,
 Oh, strange and lovely trees.
But pilgrims to your distant shrine
Would toll, oh Caribbean pine.

And caravans from far would come
 To share your loneliness,
To make swift rumors thrust and thrum
 About your loveliness.
And weary folk would hear and thrill
To know that you were living still.

That you are standing as you are,
 A sudden splendid thing,
Either branches twisting toward a star
 In beauty starting.
So strange, so rare, so half divine,
Forgive our blindness, of great pine.

Miracle.

How can a man who will not hear
Be blessed with what the winds say
 clear.

How can a man who will not live
Grow great with all the earth can
 give?

How can the power of sky or sea
Unchain the man who won't be free?

How can they? Yet from spring to spring
A few men's hearts lift, answering.

And all the silent might of these
Bear fruit from old sterilities.

Roots.

I would have communion with old roots of trees,
 Grappling with the cold earth's clayey secrecies;
I would learn their wisdom, deep underground,
Groping old root ends, what have you found?

Down in the deep earth, where old roots go,
Writhing and fingering and moving very slow.
Dreadfully feeling with painful hard toil,
Tell me now, tree roots, the meaning of the soil.

Silent are the tree roots, intimate with earth,
Wise with all the wisdom of seedtime and birth,
Sure in spite of blindness and lost sea and sun,
Gripping at the tough strength earth deeps have won.

So I have communion with old roots of trees,
Dig deep, as they do, with elbows and with knees,
Feeling through me all that still strength go,
Rock strength and earth strength. And then I'd grow.

(June 24, 1923)

ᔐ2 ᔐ South Florida Booster

The natural beauty that inspired Douglas was imperiled by a rapid growth that alarmed her. South Florida represented to her a unique tropical frontier, America's last frontier, which was disappearing beneath concrete and asphalt. Between 1920 and 1930, Miami and the surrounding Dade County area experienced the fastest population growth in the state, with a county-wide gain of 100,000 people. "What had been beautiful, a delicate balance between nature and a small population," she wrote in 1977, "I saw being destroyed by hordes of men convinced that millions were to be had by gambling with the prices of land for which they knew or cared nothing."[1] In the columns selected for this chapter, Douglas's position on the subject of rapid growth and development reflects the complexity of her thinking.

The bustle of 1920s South Florida development captivated her on more than one level. "When you grow up with a new city," she was quoted saying sixty years later, "it is extraordinary. You might not approve of everything, but at least you're there. It's life."[2] Even as she advocated preserving the indigenous beauty of South Florida, its junglelike landscape and unspoiled beaches, she supported growth in general. At the same time, she was openly critical of its wayward indirection, hastiness, destruction, and the greed and insensitivity behind it. Douglas hoped that Miami would look to the older cities of Europe for positive examples. When with the Red Cross she had been taken with the unique beauty that emanated from a city's local culture and physical setting. As a columnist, she began expressing the language of regionalism, the idea that each region should retain its own singular character by making the best of local cultural patterns and natural surroundings.[3] To the *Miami Herald* columnist, that meant preserving the tropical integrity of South Florida and developing a distinctive culture from it.

Regionalism eventually directed Douglas's attention to the Everglades, unique in the world and South Florida's most remarkable physical feature. Yet it is interesting to learn from her columns that the person who would become most closely associated with environmental protection in Florida once actually supported the drainage and commercial development of the Everglades. Put into historical context, Douglas's early views were consistent with the advanced thinking of the day's "experts." She agreed with the basic philosophy of the Progressives, those who denounced waste in natural and human resources and who supported reform, scientific management, and efficiency to advance the greater good for the larger whole.[4]

To manage its growth, to the best benefit of all its citizens, the city of Miami, she argued, should adopt these principles as policy. Managed growth to her meant preserving green space, creating tree-shaded roadways, and retaining an open view of the ocean, bays, and beaches—making the best of the region's natural beauty. She was unabashed in her opinion that South Florida had more to offer than other parts of the country.

Douglas was actually one of the region's most vocal boosters. Her boosterism, however, followed a different vein from that of the chamber of commerce and real estate developers. She was no fan of Carl Fisher, for instance, the flamboyant Indiana car salesman and Indianapolis Speedway developer who, after pioneering the process of creating land with dredge fill, remade the urban landscape with new hotels, nightclubs, houses, polo fields, shops, and palm-lined causeways.[5] Douglas was a booster who preached, often with evangelical fervor, the gospel of tropical beauty. She opposed local industrialization and instead supported a civilization built on agriculture, a "tropic agriculture" in the case of South Florida. Sometimes her zeal went too far, as when she advocated the introduction of exotic tropical plants, some of which eventually endangered indigenous growths.

Even so, Douglas was not blinded by her zeal. The effects of imported plants on the local flora were not well understood at the time, and Douglas was chiefly engaged with combating traditional practices and attitudes. Underlying her boosterism was a strong desire to get her point across. She was therefore quick to warn that what made South Florida attractive to residents and tourists could be lost in the wake of myopic planning policy and runaway development. Her words offered an appeal to logic, but they

A favorite leisure activity: spending time on the beach (she is on the right, leaning over). She confesses that she was often torn between work and going to the beach with friends. Preservation of the South Florida beaches for public use was a topic she often pursued in her column. Courtesy of Archives and Special Collections Department, Richter Library, University of Miami.

eventually failed: "I could write and write," she reflected decades after quitting her column. "No one paid attention."[6]

To Miami; On Becoming a Summer Resort.

O city fair, your summer weather
Deserves a line of type or two.
Whenever northern people gather
I'm sure their knowledge is too few.

They think 'neath tropic sun we swelter.
They think we suffer from the heat.
They think our days are but a welter
Of sun strokes and mosquitoes fleet.

When mercury in Boston rises
Ten points or so o'er ninety-eight.
When people of assorted sizes
Die because the heat's too great.

When New York subways, like a furnace,
Scorch travelers with their torrid breath.
Why do the northern people spurn us?
Why do they choose such horrid death?

Now here, when northern heat is mounting,
The trade winds, cool and steady, blow.
When northern sunstrokes exceed counting,
No deaths our records here can show.

We boast the perfect summer weather,
A nice wet sea and rattling palms.
So don't you think that, altogether,
We're justified in singing psalms?

(June 17, 1920)

It seems exceedingly difficult for northerners to get any idea of Florida's mean temperature until they get here, when they learn, to their joy, that no temperature in Florida is ever mean.

(November 16, 1920)

Everglades.

Around you there, as still you stand,
Wheels the wide windy open land,
Stretching vast arms beneath the sky
To touch horizon whistling by;
A thin, keen, gleaming saber blade,
That severs heaven from Everglades.
The green reeds ripple under breeze
Like cool lake water; clumps of trees,
Dark hammocks lift their shadowed hues
Beyond the sparkling shallow slews.
From sunrise rim to sunset gate
The lance of road thrusts white and straight,
Shocking the silence with its cry
Of empire marching westwardly.

(July 9, 1921)

Builders.

There was the jeweled green of tropic trees,
 There was the river, sparkling to the bay,
There was the crystal skies infinities
And lonely dawns of many a crystal day.
Westward, the open Glades, remote green-gray,
Eastward the radiant, shifting, sapphire sea,
Wave-wash, wind beat, bird call and silence endlessly.

Until the buzzards, circling slow, that swung,
Etched sharp and inky in the silver air,
Broke into fluttering at the clangor rung

With metal strokes upon clear metal these;
And then the shattered silence seemed more rare
Since it had passed forever. Nevermore
Such utter soundlessness should breathe along this shore.

Picks clinging, ringing as they lift and sweep,
And clattered shovels, shouting, curses, cries,
The nail-shod shoes of singing negroes keep
A steady monotone. The axes rise,
Trees crash and fall and hammers then begin
Their brick staccato, beating sharply over all the din.

Then came the linked and ringing rails of steel
Tying this outpost to the smoking towns,
And locomotives, whose long eerie squeal
Ripped through the tropic night and its soft sounds
Racing across the pinelands; iron hounds
Coursing with clamor that far-fleeing hare,
Distance that they desire, straining to snatch and tear.

That was the opening page of this, our city,
Mothered by beauty such as earth makes known,
Fathered by all the greed of men, hot, gritty,
Eager to mark this also as his own.
Unpainted shacks, tin awnings, swift had grown
Upon scarred, cleared places, ugly, cheap,
Man cannot reach great beauty with one sudden leap.

Ant hills that grow to some fine symmetry,
Corals that branch in slow and stony bloom,
Fireflies that stitch a glittering tapestry,
Follow a pattern lovely as old doom.
So all the chocked and huddled lives of men
Build in their cities beauty in spite of them.

Somehow a pattern, worked in new cement,
In brick, in pine boards and in plaster, grew,
And still the sky curved when men vehement,
Shouted and struggled and the town was new.

Much wasted effort, frothings, foamings, few
That looked beyond next week, or the week after;
And there was horseplay, lynchings, murder, love and laughter.

Masons and merchants, tailors, plumbers, ad men,
Tourists and priests and lawyers, negroes, Greeks,
Crowded the streets with good men and with bad men,
Just as spring freshets boil down empty creeks;
And where had been the jungle there were reeks
From spoiling garbage, gasoline and train smoke
And miles of roofs wetly when the rains broke.

But white and shining, whiter still and better,
The streets were carven and new walls were raised,
Spelling from out of chaos the first letter
Of all that beauty some day shall see phrased,
In spite of waste and shoddy thought and slattern
Cleaving through clutter to some hidden, half-greased pattern.

Gardens and gracious lawns and new set trees,
Swept streets and shiny, careful subdivisions,
Tuned somehow nearer to high harmonies,
A city builded of ten thousand visions,
ten thousand guesses, held against derision;
A city rising to a mighty future,
Greater than all men's dreams that gave it rapture.

Yes, we know perfectly well that we wrote that and printed it last year and
we think it is the right time to reprint it, with the new charter starting in
now and everything. And besides somebody asked us to. We forget who.
(*July 17, 1921*)

A lady who has lived in Miami for many years called us up this morning
and told us where we had overstepped our poetic license the other day in
mentioning a lynching that had occurred in Miami in the early days. She
says the point of the whole thing should have been that it was a miracle that
lynchings didn't happen, considering how much else did, but that in spite

of murders and other assorted crimes being committed, the fair name of Miami was never blotted with a lynching.

Somehow the leading citizens brought it about that the law took its course in an orderly manner, in spite of everything. We are glad to correct our careless statement, which, we will cheerfully admit, was made in the heat of the chase of rhymes. We just thought that there probably were lynchings, and let it go at that. Herein, however, is our apology to the early days.

(July 19, 1921)

We have been out with Mr. Curtis of the park department to look at some of the city parks.

Last fall the city parks were only plots of ground, with a few trees, lots of sand, and very many sandspurs. Today something seems to have happened to them. There may not be more trees, but somehow a sense of order has come upon them, and here and there a group of seedlings, and paths blocked out and men working on them, and tennis courts sketched out and men working on them, and slat houses begun and men working on them. And if you look very closely and follow Mr. Curtis's pointing finger you will see that what has happened in this year is the shaping of the outline of the future parks of the city of Miami. If the people wish it, if they wish the city of Miami—the only city of the United States in the tropics— to become known, not just by advertising signs along the road, but by the beauty of her out-of-doors, all they have to do is indicate that the park department must have more money than it has now. The parks of Miami can be famous. People from all over the United States can come here to study tropical growths, to see how tropical trees and plants and shrubs can be utilized in making the loveliest city in the world. And they will come, you know that. All that the city of Miami, Florida, needs is a public which has sense enough to recognize that her parks can be one of her very greatest assets.

That, of course, takes an extraordinary lot of common sense, because at first glance people think that what we need is factories and shops and canneries and things. The people who think that, however, haven't the farthest

sight. They overlook the fact that wherever, in any country, in any age, any sort of little old backwoods town has in some degree or other arrived at beauty, that town has become famous. Look at Athens. Nothing but a little old town in flat, green-grey country, with an abrupt hill in the middle of it covered with old stones. But because those old stones, in their ruin, are still fairly singing with the beauty their makers put into them, that city is filled with modern hotels and great wide streets and palaces and taxis today. The old stones did it.

Look at Florence. A tiny little place—Miami is bigger. The Miami river has more water in it in the summer time than the Arno has. The hills around Florence are low and grey-green and misty. There is nothing about them as breath-taking, as extraordinary, as these vast surges of white fire over the city of Miami, which we call the Gulf clouds. Florence has no sea, just beyond. Its streets are crooked and its people are often ragged. Yet Florence was and still is and will be for many years yet, because in her streets men walked who were not afraid to dream about beauty, who knew, not because they'd read it in a book, or their women folks had told them, but who knew, that to build a bell tower, a church, a baptistry, to fill a public square with great statues, was to make Florence a real place, not just a lot of houses, but a city fit to demand the loyalty of its citizens, fit to stand out for four centuries, and a place where people could go to learn what beauty is. As they do today.

Look at Chester, in England, which is thronged with visitors because its main streets have doubled arched colonnades. Look at Bruges, in Belgium, also smaller than Miami, but with a belfry and a city hall (think of it, just a city hall), and a public square so bright and lovely and fine that people come there, and stay in hotels, just to see them. And come not once, but again and again and again.

Look at Miami. A city with so many beautiful possibilities that it makes one gasp a little to think what the merchants of Venice, who built Venice, could have done with it. Think what those artist-citizens of Florence could have produced under this sky, by this sea, backed by these tremendous Everglades. Think what Baron Haussmann, who took old Paris and ruthlessly made it into a great city, could have done with Miami. Think what the

people who built the cathedral of Chartres, in France, could have produced in the way of a city hall for Miami. Think what the man who built Mount Vernon for George Washington, or the men who built the Alhambra, could have done for us.

"But," you say, "these men were great men, famous artists, sculptors, architects. We couldn't expect to be able to afford such things even if they were alive, here in Miami."

Listen. The people who made Venice beautiful were the people of Venice. They had the sheer common sense, which many Americans lack, to realize that beauty always pays. And they, the people, gave their own artists and architects and sculptors such a sense of intelligent support that the architects and sculptors not only did better, but the greatest in the world were glad and honored to be asked to work for the city of such people.

Do you think times have changed so much? Do you think it is silly to imagine that Miami cannot be beautiful with the wealth of natural, out-of-door beauty which no other city in America could rival? Then you are the one who is silly. What is more, you lack in some of the essentials of the best citizenship. For what is citizenship but to desire for our city, not for our immediate commercial advantage, but for the city as an idea, as a community where people can be happy, the best that has been known and done and thought in the world.

Is it so difficult to imagine Miami beautiful? The people who cannot imagine beauty are the people who make beauty impossible. The people who cannot see that the parks of Miami, the green places, the jungles, the whole lavish tropic setting, are the greatest assets of Miami today, are themselves limiting Miami to crudeness, to the third rate.

We need more money for the parks of Miami. We need cooperation with each other to increase an interest, not only in our parks but in our streets and our waterfronts and our own backyards. The whole future of the city, and that most certainly includes the commercial, depends on what we do with the idea.

(October 8, 1922)

Of course it goes without saying that we agree wholeheartedly with the idea that a beautiful city is its own best advertising. But we are not fully acquiescent to the opinion that the purpose of Miami is simply that of a rest cure and resort. We don't want factories. But our correspondent forgets that we are going to be a great center for exporting the products of the Everglades. You mustn't talk about Miami alone any more, you know. You can't ignore South Florida. Somehow I cannot help thinking of South Florida as a creative region, the only one of its kind in the United States, where we can raise all the remarkable lavish growths of the tropics and where may be developed the production of hundreds of things which we now import in huge quantities. We haven't even begun to find out what we can do with these Everglades. And then, too, the whole character of this South Florida is a creative one. Dr. Fairchild says that Miami can teach the whole world how to live in the tropics.[7] He believes that this region is the great laboratory region for the world, where botanical and horticultural experiments can be carried on under ideal conditions for observation. That means that South Florida will be a place where new ideas will be created. And I believe also, because we are not cramped here within walls, because we don't have to worry about cold and heat and coal and heavy clothing, about all the restrictions of northern life, but can live with the sun and the winds, that, if we choose to have it so, thought can be freer here than in many other places. We should develop into freer communities, freer personalities, living here in South Florida. We can, if we see it right, and choose to bring it about, cause South Florida to be a laboratory of another kind, a laboratory for social thinking, for social experiment, to show the world how people—just ordinary, average men and women—can best live in communities to their own greatest advantage and to the happiness of the whole. Do you think that is too much to expect of just a few square miles of our earth? A beautiful city, and a free one? I don't know. I rather like the idea of trying it.

(October 12, 1922)

It is our firm opinion, reinforced by the words of the Scientists' Committee to the Community Council, who collectively and individually, know more about the trees and shrubs of South Florida than all the rest put together, that the best thing we can do to encourage planting of this region to tropic trees is not to experiment with new things so much as to develop the ones

whose possibilities we already have. In fact, our trouble is chiefly an embarrassment of riches, because we have in these tropics such a bewildering variety to choose from. But if we begin simply with three or four, learn those, talk about them, plant them, we will do very much more practical work than experimenting wildly and without end. For that reason we want to call the attention of all people who intend planting trees this fall to the mahogany, [which] is eminently suited to planting here. Far from being a slow grower, it is a rapid one, as one of the best specimens, that on the grounds of Dr. David Fairchild, will testify. This beautiful mahogany is only four years old but it is already 60 feet high, with a shapely trunk and the most delicate green foliage. An avenue of even two-year-old mahoganies would be a joy forever. A special expedition to secure mahogany seed will be made to the Keys by Dr. John Gifford of Coconut Grove, who is one of the leading authorities in the country on the mahogany. The black olive or bucida is that beautiful tree which until recently grew in front of the Catholic church. It was falsely called white mahogany. This is especially well adapted to avenue planting in South Florida. The pongam, which Mr. Curtis of the park department is setting out, is also a quick-growing tree, with light green shiny leaves offering much shade. It can be grown from seed. The carissa is not so much a tree as a fruit-bearing shrub, used with especial effectiveness at the entrance to the Deering estate on Coconut Grove Road, where its starry white blossoms have just given way to the brilliant red of the fruit, which, incidentally, makes wonderful marmalade. For mass planting nothing could be better than the dark shiny leaves of the carissa. And if you learn those maybe we'll tell you some more sometime.

(October 17, 1922)

From the Day Book of a Journalist.

There is no getting away from it, Coconut Grove, which the South's Only [the *Miami Herald*] insists is "the center of refinement," much, I should imagine, to the wrath of its inhabitants, has an atmosphere and a charm which no other community around here has. And I think that the reason for that is that it is older and more mellow, and that the people who settled it have been content to let garages and shops and bustle come to them,

instead of going after progress. They have cultivated their gardens to such good effect, that they have planted trees and set out vines on old walls, and kept intact, successfully, the tangles and by-paths, that they are now where many another community around here is just beginning to realize that it ought to be in another ten years. And in a full moon, with a gleam and glitter of the bay beyond Coconut Grove, and the friendly road which runs through it becomes enchanted country, where the ink-black leaf patterns are cut by moon whiteness out of white, where each orange leaf pools its separate and particular moon gleam and where the vines and the dark lift of the trees to the quicksilver skies are swept by such murmurings and rustlings as Pan alone knows the cause of through all the Pixie-led night. Enchanted country, oh, very enchanted country.

(November 6, 1922)

The Realtor

I think the realtor has come to Miami to stay,
To put the price of houses up and warn the wolf away;
And keep the tourists all amused and fill the business streets
With offices where "House for Sale" or "Lovely Bargain" greets
Your eye at every other turn until the day is done.
They seem to like their dreadful trade. It brings them lots of
 mon.
A-luring of their customers and driving them about—
For the realtors will get you
If
 you
 don't
 watch
 out.
Once there was a wealthy soul, didn't want to buy,
Called by all the businessmen a hard-boiled guy.
He only came to Florida to breathe the climate in,
And watch the hotel people taking other tourists' tin,
But they called on him at breakfast and they phoned him after
 tea,

And they made his landless state of mind one lingering agony.
Until he bought a bay front—and then quickly sold it out—
So, the realtors will get you
If
 you
 don't
 watch
 out.
Long time ago the people used to laugh and sneer and grin
And talk about how Florida kept taking suckers in.
But once they come and see the place they always change their
 song,
And seem to think that Florida will be great stuff ere long.
So when you see them platting out a sub-div-i-sion
You'd better mind your bank account and go and get your gun,
For the value always rises just as soon as it's sold out—
And the realtors will get you
If
 you
 don't
 watch
 out.
(November 7, 1922)

The New York schools are getting so crowded that they are going to use the public parks for physical exercises and setting-up drills. Strikes us that is a very sensible idea and might well be employed by Miami. Really, we can't see why all outdoors isn't a good place to hold classes down here, with a roof to dash under occasionally when it rains. We are so wedded to our northern ideas of roofs and walls and ceilings when we get down here that it takes some time for us to realize that this is a different country and differ-ent conditions. All we need is a floor, a roof and some wire screening and we can forget about storm doors and sodding the cellar. All we need, really, is a change from a near frigid to a tropical attitude of mind.

(November 10, 1922)

Every once in so often we get a chance to ride out in the country, or down to Coconut Grove or out to Larkins or somewhere, just about sunset, when the whole sky is blaring bronze and molten copper behind the clotted black lace of the Caribbean pine trees, and we wonder all over again why anybody with eyes in his head can talk about any other trees but the Caribbean pine as the meaning and symbol of South Florida. The more you see of them the lovelier they are. People think they are dreary, or monotonous, or at least, they don't think at all. Heavens, monotonous! They are as monotonous as a black lace shawl, as dreary as the most wonderful Gothic wood carving, as stupid as fretted black ivory, as unstimulating as the work of the most delicate and most sensitive artists in the world, as uninteresting as etchings, as lacework, as frostwork. They are utterly unique to South Florida. People who say they see these trees in the other southern states are quite wrong. The Caribbean pine begins in Florida, south of Fort Lauderdale, and we will defy people to prove that it is the same, or even looks the same, as the long leaf yellow pine to the northwards. It is South Florida, it means South Florida, and if people will only give up a few of their preconceived notions about what this country ought to be like, and really see its charm for what it really is, we will much sooner begin to develop its picturesque side properly. We will continue to dispense hatred, wrath, superiority and scorn every time we pass a real estate subdivision that advertises in this very paper that it is to be "landscaped" when the work has been begun by clearing off every pine on the place. The people who cut down pine trees for actual necessity are the sort of people who—well, they are the sort of people who cut down pine trees. That's pretty bad.

(November 11, 1922)

Just why this particular part of the globe, as flat as the horizon which circles it, is not called "The Land of the Sky," in the place of those hilly countries where the sky in sight is only a segment of the sky, and where the sheer protuberant mass of the land gets in the way of its greatest sweep and height and extent, we have never been able to guess. Yet every little hill country speaks of its sky with a proprietorial sort of pride, and the flat countries, like ourselves, in particular, are taught to be meek because we are lowly, quite

ignoring the fact that here sky has no obstruction and that here the cloud formations, because of the Gulf and the temperature and the ocean or whatever else, are a more stupendous and shifting panorama, daily and hourly, than all the hill countries put together. To wake up any morning and be able to look out as far as the eye will, across lacy pinelands with their bigness, their fine open sweep, and then to ascend with a leap of genuine emotion to a range of shouting cloud mountains, whiter than all whiteness, dazzling with such pearly intensity in the morning sun and the free air that they are a veritable exaltation, that is to know the sky and the great reach of the earth, as no hills, however imposing, can give it.

Of course, to hill people, that is blasphemy, but why worry about the hill people? We are a sea people, and a flat earth people, and it is high time that we were learning a little natural pride in the tremendous mountains of dazzle which move and shift and change over our heads. If we don't, who will?

It is strange how quickly some people get used to uniqueness, so that they constantly yearn for the things which are beyond their horizon, when, in this most exotic, most strange, most adventurous strip of country left in the United States, they can see only the surface, and declare it uninteresting.

(November 12, 1922)

The New Spirit.

How shall we find re-birth from tired nations.

Or a great cry from weary people?

Why should we look far off for the seeds of the new coming?

Here is South Florida of the sea and of the sky;

Here is South Florida, wide, vibrant, abundant;

Here men and women may breath deep of the salt air;

Here men and women may bare their heads in sunshine.

If there are seeds of a new coming, they are here with us.

South Florida, South Florida,

In you are the first whispers of renascence!

(November 23, 1922)

We were talking, a while ago, about the new words which the Community Council had added to our vocabulary. We talked about "civic courtesy," which is the new word of the Civitan Club, and about "biological living," which the Woman's Club seems to be interested in, but we talked especially and particularly about that word "regional," which we are all using, and which is not the special province of any of the clubs of the Community Council because it belongs to all of them. Perhaps the Kiwanis, who are in charge of the conservation work, and who, through their chairman, Judge Smathers, have been holding up the hands of the park department so valiantly, are more interested in it than most. But still I insist that "regional" belongs to us all. That is why one of the very newest phases of this regional idea has given us another few words. In addition to "regional" we have "the new geography." "The new geography" deals with what is called "regional geography" as opposed to "political geography." There is something new here, isn't there?

Regional geography, we have just learned, provides the background for political geography. Stop to think about it. The most important thing to us, the one factor which colors and shapes our lives and has always colored and shaped the lives of man, is this wrinkled old earth under our feet. You cannot ignore it. You cannot get away from it. In considering any city, or any county or any region. As we are constantly considering South Florida, you cannot begin with economics or industries, you cannot begin with people, you cannot begin with groups or societies or systems of government or anything else, until you have first considered the earth on which the whole rests and which conditions everything. "The new geography" holds that geography and botany, not in general, but the detailed geography and botany of the region itself, is the fundamental study, not just in teaching geography in schools, but for any development, physical, social or any other way. Geography and botany, geography and botany, those are your fundamentals. That is why we have harped so much upon our botany, upon our trees and shrubs and flowers, because they are the inevitable background from which we get, not just pleasure, but food, clothing and shelter. The geography and the botany of South Florida are the two most important studies for any development of South Florida.

You remember that word "ecology?" That meant the proper fitting of plant to environment, "bringing the plant to the land" in our Mr. Sim-

mons' excellent phrase. Wherever people have tried to force this county of South Florida to do something it couldn't there has been disaster. You cannot bring the land to the plant. But now we are taking time to look about us, to study, really study, our soil, our climate and the other geographic conditions, we are discovering a thousand marvelous things, plants that are indigenous to India and China and Africa, fruits and vegetables, medicinal herbs and condiments now being imported to America at great expense, take to a life here in tropic South Florida as if they had never known anything else. We simply must begin with our geography, our regional geography. Do you see?

(December 21, 1922)

And then this weather, this inimitable, sparkling, snappy golden and peacock weather, isn't it wonderful? Aren't you glad you live in Miami? Aren't you glad you came? Would you trade a single hour of these vibrant, salt, fragrant afternoons for a whole day of blizzard? Isn't this tender deep sky, with creamy new cloud puffs nothing short of miracle, but an enduring one? And the sea, lime green and jade and jasper and foaming, cool and roaring way from the horizon? And the bay, with the white boats, and the gulls like flakes of snow rising and falling? And the wind beating at the shining leaves of coconuts? And in the honeyed warmth of the sun on your shoulders and the fresh sweet air in your face? And the feeling of bustle and drive and hurry and crispness along Flagler Street? And new people coming in and looking at everything with bright eyes? And the automobile tags from everywhere and Honolulu? And the hotel piazzas filling up? And the smart new things in the shop windows? And the nights—oh, my goodness, these nights! Don't you like living after all?

(December 26, 1922)

We are a frontier city and we are the last frontier city. This is the heart of the last wilderness, the place to which the last Indians were driven, who fought for their liberty, the place last to be developed in the United States. When the lavish riches of our wilderness here shall have been conquered there will never be any more frontier in the United States of America.

We believe that the things that are true for us in South Florida are true for America. We see ourselves as pioneers, just as the first Americans were. We see ourselves as immigrants, who have come here from everywhere else, for all the various reasons which affected our ancestors. Some of us have come seeking health, and have found a new place to be loyal to. Some of us have come seeking freedom from different conditions, and have found a finer freedom to work for. Some of us have come looking for personal advancement, and have found a great new region whose advancement has come to seem greater than our own. From all sorts and kinds of reasons we have come here, but we stay because we believe tremendously in this place and in its future, not just in a material way, but somehow related to this freedom and health and happiness which men are constantly seeking.

(December 29, 1922)

People need not fear about the future of South Florida especially on such days as these. They talk about "climate," but it is more than climate. It is something great and fine and young that the land possesses, something that is really a sort of elixir of life, of the sort that old Ponce de Leon sought for, and which men have come seeking ever since. They talk about this country being enervating. Enervating? Huh! This sort of weather has more pep in it than all of New York and Chicago put together. There you have to move lively to keep from freezing to death. Here you move lively and work lively and even think lively, because it is the very tempo of the place. The big sweep of it, the openness, the high skies, the sea, all of it will someday, I am very sure, produce a breed of people who will be freer in their minds and in their living than the harassed, wall-ridden people of the north. Why not? We all know perfectly well that there is such a thing as the influence of climate on character. That is undisputed. And the character of this climate is unmistakable. It is nothing that people tell you. You feel it, whenever you hit this place. In three days you wonder what has happened to you. You can't help feeling happier and lighter and gayer. Oh, you may make yourself unhappy. You may make yourself completely miserable. You always have that privilege. But if you will really let the country seep into the marrow of your bones, you will find that it has a tremendous something to give you.

(December 21, 1922)

It is pleasant to see how the newspapers of South Florida are calling it "South Florida," just like that, with a capital "s." Whether the politicians like it or not, and in no relation at all to legislative measures, there is a South Florida, a distinct, different, unified section of country, growing more and more like-minded every day.

(January 29, 1923)

Instead of every bit of its land for cultivation the county officials recognize that the hammock lands of Lake County are spots of rare and unusual beauty which must be preserved for future generations. These beautiful bits of jungle are fast disappearing before the grubbing hoe and if they are kept, as they certainly should be, now is the time to do it. Lake County seems to have some unusually intelligent and far-sighted officials, for they have set aside a large tract of this hammock land as a reservation, never to be touched, no matter how valuable from the point of view of raising flowers for perfumery they may become. The United States has already lost too much of great natural beauty, of which the succeeding generations will be permanently cheated, to allow our own Florida jungles completely to be swept away. We must realize what they really mean, as the only genuine tropic jungles in America, the most truly tropic things we have, containing a wealth of growth which may some day bear seeds of tremendous import to us commercially. Around Miami, also, the jungles are fast disappearing and it is a shame that we have only the tiny but very beautiful Jungle Park retained before the encroachments of subdivisions and the people who like to destroy a whole jungle in order to smooth the land off and plant red hibiscus and acalypha alternating with Australian pine and coconut palms. Lake County has set a pace which all of Florida could well emulate. They are doing real work in county planning, while we only talk about it.

(January 31, 1923)

We find the power of the United State constantly becoming more and more federalized, the central government more and more in control, with that delicate balance between the states and the federal government, on which rests political democracy, being shattered. The complaint constantly arises from our thinking men that we are becoming more and more a na-

tion ruled by bureaus. And it is true, of course, politically. But there is another movement on foot which they do not recognize, but which undoubtedly will be the solution to the problem. They do not recognize it because they really cannot think in any terms but political ones, and the new movement is a movement in people's thought, in their manner of thinking. It is the movement which we are learning to call regionalism, or regional development, or which Vachel Lindsay calls "the new localism." It concerns itself with making people of a locality more conscious of the unique possibilities of that locality, with bringing back to the local region the interest and the development which has gone heretofore to the great cities or abroad. It is developing local people and painters and writers. It is teaching people, all over again, to enjoy the richness of their own boundaries, to develop intensively, beginning with their own roots and their own soil. Thank goodness, this movement is not political. But it will be the salvation of a real democracy, nevertheless.

(February 5, 1923)

We don't know exactly how to do it, or how to phrase it emphatically enough, or viciously enough, but it is obviously up to some one to impress upon the minds of the buyers of property in what used to be known as Brickell Hammock that the jungle growth which covers that land ought to be, as far as possible, preserved. The tendency is to buy a lot and clear it clean of all growth, and then set out palms and hibiscus, whether they are suited to that land or not. Yet we must get it through our heads, all of us, that that jungle land is unique to South Florida. Nowhere else in the entire United States can a real tropic jungle be seen. It can grow nowhere else. And to wantonly destroy it for building purposes and with a mistaken idea of development, is to wipe out one of the greatest factors of our regional life. The Amazon jungles are worth traveling miles to see. People spend thousands of dollars and endure all sorts of hardships to study tropic growths in tropic jungles all over the world. And yet here at our very doors are such jungles in miniature where dozens of almost unknown species are already growing, where orchids are at home, and where the whole striving, tangled, fascinating phenomenon of jungle life goes on daily, before our blind eyes. To destroy utterly these jungles, is to do something that no individual has a right to do, no matter how clear his title to the actual land on

which this jungle grows. Individual rights are all very well, but the preser-
vation of these jungles, in some sort of way, is a duty which we owe to the
entire region. I do not mean for a moment that lots in hammock land
should not be cleared and houses built. That would be unreasonable. But at
least we all have a right to ask that the clearing be done intelligently, that
the jungle be thinned out with an eye to the preservation of the most inter-
esting specimens, and with a realization of the actual dollars-and-cents
value of this growth, over the palms which ordinarily are set out. And, if
you will notice, royal palms or even coconut do not seem to do so well on
this cleared land. I have seen a stand of royal which looks already as if they
were not long for this world. The requirements for the growth of royals are
not fulfilled in this particular situation. We must recognize the importance
of this consideration. How can one find words strong enough to make
people realize it? Won't you think up some blistering ones for us?

(February 6, 1923)

We have been asked why it is that there seems to be so little background of
music and art and poetry here in Miami, when there are so many people
striving to create it. The background of a mellow ancient culture which is
found in places in New England or Pennsylvania or even in the older estab-
lished places in the West is lacking to us here. Of course, the old excuse that
we are so young, that the region is so much of a frontier, is always good. Yet
the people who come here, many of them, come from an older culture and
yet seem not to have been able to establish that quality here. I think the
answer lies in another thing beside our newness. I think the difficulty is
that the older cultures always have difficulty in transplanting themselves so
as still to prove stimulating in a region where the conditions are so unique
and different and where the problem is as much one of regional develop-
ment as of intellectual development. The creative force in America has al-
ways thrown itself into the building of new places, rather than the creation
of art. That is, until the new places became old places. Art was then a de-
tached, leisurely luxury. But the more I know of this South Florida, the
more it seems to me that the opportunity for creating a great new art lies in
our development of the country. South Florida should be our art, more
than just a frontier. Our music and painting and poetry must first find it-
self in South Florida soil . . . as a genuine stimulant to the imaginations of

a creative people. That way, we will have not just backgrounds of art, but foregrounds of more beautiful living. It is the architects and the city and county planners and the landscape architects who have first attacked their problem. The province of the other arts must do likewise. This is not only what South Florida needs, it is what America needs, and the time is coming, or is here, when the poets and the musicians and the painters are beginning to recognize it.

(March 3, 1923)

It is with great regret that we notice the erection of huge billboards facing the approaches to the Flagler Street bridge. The Miami River, let alone, and not smeared all over with atrocities, is a really beautiful thing. The park department is doing all that it can to beautify the city park and the bit of river bank which belongs to it. Yet if these billboards are to be allowed to take up all the bank adjoining the river, it might just as well be some hideous New England mill town. It is obviously to the advantage of the sign company that these billboards have such an eligible location. But if it is dollars and cents in Miami's pocket to be a beautiful city, then surely there should be a public opinion strong enough to protest against such billboards. The view down Flagler Street to the bay was ruined by the enormous cheap structures of the electric sign over Elser's pier, and now apparently the rest of it is to be made as bad. There remains only the Royal Palm park, which would undoubtedly be an excellent place for billboards also. And when we get the bay front park there will be another. If we are going to be a billboard town we might as well be prepared for it.

This town spends all sorts of money advertising its unique beauty, and yet here we are, breaking our necks to cheapen everything we have. In another two thousand years, they tell us, man may become a sensible animal.

(March 7, 1923)

That phase of city planning which is commonly known as the zoning system is designed for the protection of the city as regards health, convenience, beauty, comfort and safety. The day has passed when people will agree that it is good practice to jam up a store or factory alongside a church or a residence. There is something in the eternal fitness of things that causes

a feeling of rebellion against such a procedure. No city could ever become attractive under such conditions; that is the reason why so many communities have come to a realization of the fact that it is possible to have the desirable things in civic life instead of those things that are undesirable and why, today, more than fifteen million people live in zoned cities, towns and villages, according to government statistics. The main purpose of zoning is to keep our incongruous features from residential sections, such as garbage, factories, stores, warehouses and manufacturing plants.

(March 8, 1923)

It is a great comfort to us personally that the greatest development of South Florida is to be agricultural. Of course those who have never been west of Lawrence Drive will be astonished at the word since it is the popular opinion that all we can raise in South Florida is what the preachers call hell, and room rent for tourists. But anyone who has been penetrating those vast acres of rich black soil which lie between Miami and the Gulf of Mexico knows that those thousands and thousands of square miles guarantee to South Florida a future founded on the realest thing there is, the earth. But it is a comfort to us because we believe wholeheartedly that a civilization built upon agriculture is a richer and finer and more interesting thing than that built upon the mills and factories of the industries. Let city folks in white kid gloves sneer as they like, the finest things are done where there is a close relation to the soil. Where the people have lived with the earth you will find great poetry, great art, great and fruitful civilizations. Where cities have absorbed the attention of the people to such an extent that they have become parasitic, the civilization has become rotten and the life of the nation has been endangered. The herds and the flocks of primitive peoples, the open fields, the wide meadows, the gardens, the bees, the well-tilled farms, have been recorded in the writings of all races. They give something to the heart of mankind that pavements cannot. The greatest thing that we in South Florida can hope for is a mutual and equal development of city and country, a city beautiful and healthful and free, giving stimulus and focus for the life of the country, a splendidly developed countryside giving background and purpose and meaning for the city, with equal respect and mutual understanding. That is what our agricultural development is going to mean.

(March 9, 1923)

It seems to me that this year will be marked upon the annals of South Florida as the year when the people became more and more vividly aware of the Everglades. The rains of last fall were a blessing, since they fixed our attention upon these tremendous black prairies between us and the Gulf of Mexico. They produced activity in drainage matters which already insures success of the project of drainage. And as a result you find everybody nowadays talking "Everglades." That is as it should be. The wealth of South Florida, but even more important, the meaning and the significance of South Florida, lies in the black muck of the Everglades and the inevitable development of this country to be the great tropic agricultural center of the world. That insures to us forever that we will be the sort of region which a cheap industrialism cannot touch, but which rightly planned and developed as agricultural, can produce not just wealth, but a social structure of value and integrity, a civilization, or at least let us work to that end, rich in all of the things which makes the life of any man interesting and significant and mellow and valuable.

(March 20, 1923)

When the scientists' committee of the Community Council first got together to make out a list of trees which were good for streets and parks and boulevards in South Florida, they named the albizzia lebbek as one of the most important and interesting. You can call it albizzia for short but its other name is woman's tongue. This is to remind you that you must not forget the albizzia. It is one of the most rapidly growing trees we have. It is a beautiful shade tree and, according to the description, has pinnate leaves slightly resembling the Circassian bean. It is one of the most commonly grown avenue trees in Egypt, a five-mile avenue of them leading to the Great Pyramid from Cairo. The best specimen of this tree in South Florida is Dr. [Charles Torrey] Simpson's wonderful seventeen-year-old albizzia which easily looks as if it might be fifty years old, judging from northern standards. Albizzia lebbeks planted along our country roads would make high tunnels of the thinnest, laciest, softest green in the world and provide against the glare from the tropical sun which is one of the first objections which northern people make against South Florida. Very respectfully, we suggest that such subdivisions as Hollywood would be greatly benefited by a splendid stand of albizzias.

(April 3, 1923)

Everglades.
I have seen as in a vision
the immense and illimitable Everglades,
Vast, westward lying.
Their soil is as the flesh of a new being.
Through those eternal acres a thrill runs.
The kite whirling and turning the exquisite spirals of its flight
Moves screaming before it.
Little tremblings of brown slough water runs in its by-ways.
The moccasin is disturbed by it and slips darkly westward.
Over the immense and the untouched calm of its soil
Shivers a meaning.
What is this new thing to which the Everglades listen,
Soul of the silence of the sea from which they have come,
Bone and sinew of sun to which they have been raised, a
 mighty offering and sacrifice,
But the tremor of a state of marching upon its solitudes,
But the intuition of illimitable harvests to come,
Hints of fruition.
Out of the Everglades
Vast, westward lying,
What hint and what promises already are astir
But the hints of greatness,
But the promise of maturity,
But the birth pains of a new great state to be joined to the
 marching legions of these other states,
Youth of the tropics,
Energy out of newness.
Oh, I tell you, I have seen the force of the tremendous and
 everlasting Everglades.
I have seen the black force and the sun force of its soil
Casting forever new forces among the assemblages of nations.
Through them I have seen the meaning of the new Florida,
From which she shall rise, through which she shall celebrate
 herself.
And if there are any who will belittle the vision of this Florida
I tell you they are only belittling themselves.
If they have contempt for the possibility of her greatness

I tell you they themselves are contemptible.
By no cheapening shall these Everglades be cheapened.
Let them be walled about with titles, loans, mortgages, papers,
 trivialities.
They shall remain inviolable and themselves.
They shall give themselves tremendously and still be virgin.
They shall lend themselves to the crooked scheming of
 schemers
And remain untouched.
I have seen as in a vision this thing about the Everglades,
Meaning and grandeur,
Beauty and terror and hugeness,
But most the ultimate life-thing,
Earth-thing,
Sea-thing,
Sun-thing,
Thing of eternal male and female,
Eternal creation.
True always to a law and a road which is ours to follow.
True for Florida.
True for you and me who shall know Florida through them,
True for the ends of the earth to which these Everglades
Eternally shall send new and immense meanings of minds and
 the livings of you and me.

(April 6, 1923)

The Tamiami Trail.

The East Coast Speaks to the West Coast.
We have watched the west for the faint, far line,
Of your dauntless feet through the swamp and the pine.
We have reached our hands in a thin white track,
West through the hammock land, west through the black,
The deep black muck and the grey great soil
And the lines have met by your toil, our toil,

Carving at the distance that is sharp and clear,
Hacking at the ramparts of the last frontier.
Today we are shouting, "Brother, brother,
Sons as we are of the same great mother."
Right hand and left hand, with Glades between,
Four hundred million acres of virgin green,
Shaped to be made into destiny.
And we cry to you toiling, "We will join you there
Where the eagles float in the hot, bright air,
Where the sky and earth shall hear our hail,
There, we shall meet you in the trail, the trail,
The first thin line that our hands shall prove,
Ours, by the might that the trade winds move,
Ours, by gulf and by sea and by sun,
Ours, by the vision we have dared and won."
Can't you hear the sobbing? Of our dredge by night?
Can't you see the gleaming of our empire light?
Isn't that the ringing of your pick and steel?
Isn't that the shudder of your dynamite we feel?
Hail, oh brave hands we have long desired.
Hail, oh strong hearts by this vastness fired.
Here we shall pledge you, we will make it true,
for we are the East. We are brother to you.
We shall not fail you, we shall not fail,
By the truth of the greatness of the gifts of the trail.
West Coast and East Coast, whom Everglades sever,
Shout—West, we are East. We are one, hence, forever.

We were more pleased than we know how to say the other day when Mr. Green of the Realty Board was ready to take up the question of proper tree, shrub and vine planting. Because it is definitely the affair of all real estate men that they should be intelligent about the plants that are growing on their land, and the plants which could grow there. The advertising possibilities alone of land on which rare tropical trees are grown are unexcelled. And that the Realty Board should recognize this seems to me a very great step forward for the best possible development for South Florida. The list of trees which we recommended to him is that list prepared by Dr. David

Fairchild, Mr. Charles Torrey Simpson, Mr. Simmons of the Plant Intro-
duction station, Dr. John Gifford and Mr. Thomas Norris for the Miami
Community Council. That list, which gives the ten best for park planting,
the ten best for boulevard planting, and so on, was compiled for them by
Mr. Reginald V. Waters. Copies of this list may be had from him. It is an
invaluable thing and one which needs no recommendation from us, since
the men who gave their time and years of study to making it are the greatest
experts in America on tropical arboriculture. The list is free to all.

(April 16, 1923)

It has always been an illusion of mine that they had wonderful sunsets in
Los Angeles. And yet I couldn't see how they could possibly have any love-
lier ones than we do. Now, imagine with what rejoicing, I learn that they
don't. To have wonderful sunsets you have to have clouds and as it doesn't
rain nine months in the year in Los Angeles naturally you don't have re-
markable sunsets. Quod erat demonstrandum. Oh, the poor things—no
sunsets? No lovely bronze and scarlet explosions behind black pine trees?
No immense and silent configurations in which the very air is tinder to the
sun's dying fire and the gold goes streaking and flashing and flaming clear
to the zenith, with ineffable strips of lavender and apple green between, and
dripping down the curve of the highest sky in rose lights and purple after-
glows that make the whole world different and eery and enchanted? Oh,
the poor things.

(April 18, 1923)

Better than a gasoline tax, for our state roads, if we may be permitted to be
fiscal for a moment, would be the tax which New York state is advocating,
a tax to the square inch on billboards. We are getting so many of them
throughout the state that they would easily pay for the road upkeep. Fine
idea, what?

(April 19, 1923)

In fact, now we think of it, we do not believe we have paid enough atten-
tion to the eating possible to do in this region. Our belief in regional devel-

opment extends to that. For in any country that you may find yourself in there is always one . . . dish which is the masterpiece of the locality, which should be eaten in the locality, cooked in the locality, caught in the locality. One should eat swordfish steaks and oysters in Boston to know what is good, just as one should eat bouillabaisse in Marseilles, and fried octopuses in Naples and Rhode Island johnnycake in Rhode Island and maple syrup in Vermont and scrapple in Pennsylvania and pork sausage in Georgia and pralines in New Orleans and—oh, well, finish it yourself. You get the idea.

Now what should we do in South Florida, for good eating and special dishes? Of course you could begin with a fruit cocktail, grapefruit and sliced mango. Then you could have broiled mangrove snapper. Ever eat any mangrove snapper, by the way? You can't get it in many of the fish markets but it's delicious. Or this dish of baked land crabs, if it turns out to be good. With grits, I suppose. And a salad of that edible palm cabbage and coconut jelly and black mangrove or orange flower honey and coffee raised from Mr. Johnston's coffee bean. That's not so bad, is it? Or are there any special South Florida dishes that we are passing up?

Oh, yes, my gracious yes. The dasheen. Did you ever have French-fried dasheen? My dear, it's delicious. You get one of those little cross-cutting graters or whatyoucallem's and just slice it down and fry it the way you fry potatoes. The effect is tremendous. You can eat them as vegetables or almost as pastry. If some enterprising restaurant were to serve some of these South Florida dinners once in a while, the dasheen certainly should be on the menu card.

And the more you think of it, the more you realize that when the tropical plant introduction station at Chapman Field really gets underway, we can almost sustain life down here for a long time without worrying about outside resources.

(April 20, 1923)

When Denman Fink, at the City Planning conference the other day said our slogan "It's June in Miami" was a clever thing, but we couldn't very well take the credit for making it so, he hit home. We wiggled and everybody else around us wiggled. For it is perfectly true. We brag about our climate,

but after all, we didn't make it. The Lord did. We don't brag about our narrow streets, but we did make them. The Lord didn't. I think it would be pleasant if we really could get together and create a city we could brag about, as our own handiwork. Then we would be justified in our boasting.

(May 11, 1923)

Perhaps it is our great national belief that the best is the most expensive which is the fault. The nature of our civilization makes the possession of large sums of money the only apparent standard of excellence, and the purchasing power of money, it seems to many of us, is utterly unlimited. Given money enough, we are made to feel, great art, beautiful living, rich and full and abundant experience, may be bought. Yet the truth is, that they cannot. The richest man in the world could command no beauty if there were not artists who thought more of their art than of his money. The most expensive pictures, houses, carpets, dinners, are not by any means the best. You cannot tell the quality by the price tag. And the question is, how are we to make that belief prevail?

(May 28, 1923)

A Journey.

I went up to Ft. Lauderdale in lovely summer weather.
I went up to Ft. Lauderdale, and oh, the air was sweet.
But oh, my heart—and oh, my eyes, on all roads altogether
Were billboards and acalypha on each side of the street.
From here to Little River's just a breezy bit of going
From here to Little River—sing hey, the jolly ride.
But oh, my sacred Uncle Sam, there's one place where there's
 growing
Three kinds of red and purple things and pink ones just beside.

From Little River to Arch Creek the trees were green and
 shady.
From Little River to Arch Creek, and, oh, the lovely stream.
But billboards, billboards everywhere, and oh, my goodness, lady,
Hibiscus and acalypha to make you, writhe and scream.

From Arch Creek to Hollywood the wind was fresh and
blowing,
From Arch Creek up to Hollywood, and oh, the day was
bright.
But oh, the treeless avenues with cement blocks growing,
And bare and flat and blistering and white and white and
white.

From Hollywood to Dania the groves and trees were splendid.
From Hollywood to Dania, with flame trees here and there.
But oh, that tin signs tacked to trees could be torn off and
ended
And subdivisions not be stripped to look so bleak and bare.

From Dania to Ft. Lauderdale the road is smooth and cheery,
From Dania to Ft. Lauderdale, and oh, the meadowlarks.
And river running by great oaks, but goodness gracious dearie,
They're selling lots in Lauderdale that should be kept for parks.

I went up to Ft. Lauderdale in lovely summer weather.
I came back from Ft. Lauderdale, and oh, the stars were bright.
Now I'm not really quite so cross and critical together,
But when we start this building why don't we do it right?

(June 9, 1923)

Now that the election is all over and the city commissioners are resuming
their work, we take this opportunity of saying all over again that among
other things this town needs badly is an Advisory Park Commission. The
duties of the park department superintendent are growing so great, and are
of such diverse character, that he needs very badly a group of citizens who
shall act in an advisory capacity, who can look over his plans and approve
them, who can bring expert advice to his assistance. The parks of Miami
should be one of its greatest assets. We are an outdoor, tropical city, and our
parks should be known all over the country for their unique beauty. They
will attract winter visitors. They will make Miami a summer resort as well
as a winter resort. The interest being shown in parks and park development
all over Florida indicates that at last the people are recognizing how much

the future success of Florida cities depends upon them. We need an Advisory Park Commission. They don't need to be paid. There are plenty of citizens who know about planting who will be glad to serve for nothing. The charter doesn't need to be altered. We need a park commission, Mr. City Commissioners. How about it?

(June 10, 1923)

It would be a wise thing if a customer for a city lot were to ask the real estate agent for it if he's planted any trees on his own property yet.

(June 15, 1923)

Sand in Your Shoes.
*(There is a tradition in South Florida which says that
anyone who once gets his shoes full of Florida sand will
never be entirely happy in any other place.)*
Sand in your shoes?
Ah, you're caught,
Entranced, trapped, magicked, like the rest of us.
Now, you'll never be quite free again,
Now, though you tread your northern pavements,
Though all your green hills call you,
The elm ways, or the golden prairies of the west,
Topped by far mountains,
All these will seem a little alien.
Sand in your shoes?
Our country's fist, flat as your hand,
Monotonous with rampart ranks of pine,
Palmetto scrub. No hills, no valleys,
Only sky, sea and tropic earth.
But you will lift your head to listen,
back in your north, for rustlings of a palm tree.
Over the roaring streets, for sound of soft seawater,
Breaking and flashing under such a sun as never north has
 seen.

The airs, hereafter, will seem harsh to you,
There will be something, something that you lack,
Some sense of lovely living,
Some soft breath,
Some stinging color,
Flame trees and turquoise sky,
A peacock sea, and sunsets.
Explosions, gold, bronze, brass, and crimson,
And a moon thereafter, to drown you in white magic.
Then this city, this sudden thing, this motley, this Miami,
Somehow a-stir with beauty,
Beauty in spite of itself,
Building because it has to build, because of something,
Some spirit, feeling, call it what you will
That catches men and stabs them
So that they have to build.
Oh, it's magic, magic. So I warn you
 You're caught.
Shake out your shoes and dust them,
Tread lightly.
Still the sand will cling.
We'll get you yet.
 Laugh, if you like, but just wait and see.

(June 17, 1923)

Over in Europe they have discovered a way of bottling sunlight and we trust that our energetic Chamber of Commerce has already made arrangements for making it another Miami product.

(June 22, 1923)

↬3↫ *Political Analyst*

It is difficult to imagine Douglas not having an opinion on politics, public policy, or even foreign policy. The Galley provided an ideal rostrum from which to give her take on such matters.

Douglas got her first personal taste of politics in 1917 when she and other suffragists lobbied state legislators in Tallahassee. She was disgusted by the indifference, chauvinism, and crudeness of the so-called "wool-hat boys." Florida's legislature at the time was dominated by a conservative coalition of North Florida lawmakers with provincial attitudes.[1] Douglas, by contrast, fit into the mold of a Progressive, one who favored government intervention in the form of legislation and governmental agencies to improve the conditions of society for the disadvantaged and to protect the average citizen against the exploitative pursuits of uncaring business interests.[2] At the same time, she argued for limited governmental bureaucracy, viewing it as part and parcel of the spoils of the political party in power. Politicians, Douglas came to believe, were for the most part self-serving. On the state and national levels, the two major political parties looked out for their own collective interest rather than that of their constituents. One party was little more than a mirror of the other, as Douglas saw it, ignoring issues of public concern and leaving voters with limited choices. By the 1920s, she had lost patience with party politics and the former suffragist stopped voting.

But there was much in politics to talk about, and Douglas did. She preferred an enduring style of political commentary that was incisive in its use of sarcasm. Her allusion below to the role of the Ouija board in national politics, for instance, presaged the expression voodoo economics of the 1980s. Generally, she was cynical about the whole affair of politics, but her observations inspired many humorous one-liners. One of her favorite po-

Douglas in the 1980s giving one of the many speeches she made as an environmental activist. She never pulled her punches when she thought public policy and politicians warranted criticism, a trait she first revealed as writer of The Galley. Courtesy of Florida State Archives.

litical subjects was the presidential race of 1920 between Warren G. Harding, James Cox, and Eugene Debs, which Harding won. Journalists, including Douglas, enjoyed lampooning the Republican senator from Ohio for mispronouncing words and creating new ones.

Douglas, who later in life was candid about her love of an evening cocktail, also took her share of humorous jabs at the national prohibition of alcohol. The year that she stopped writing her column, the Eighteenth Amendment had been in effect for over three years, and it was proving to be a miserable failure.

On the subject of world peace, Douglas was less inclined to be humorous. She had witnessed at first hand the horrible destruction of World War I and sympathized with the people of Europe, former enemies and allies alike, while the squabbling of world leaders delayed relief for the homeless

and the starving. Congress never allowed the United States to join the League of Nations, an international organization designed to prevent another world war and championed by President Woodrow Wilson. The U.S. did come to an agreement with other world powers on self-imposed restrictions on building large warships. Douglas, nevertheless, was dubious about permanent peace. The isolationists and industrialists who were responsible for the passage of the 1922 tariff imposing heavy restrictions on imported foreign goods particularly incensed her. She recognized, even if they did not, that the tariff inflicted an undue hardship on war-torn countries trying to regain the economic stability required to feed and pacify their populations.

As a columnist, Douglas came to know the nature of the beast: the self-serving politicians and their politics. It was a knowledge that served her well when as an environmentalist she found herself dealing directly with governmental powers and the personalities behind them. She berated policymakers late in the century just as she had done in the 1920s. The beast, it seemed, had not changed its spots.

The equivalent to the old problem of the irresistible force and immovable body has been found. It is the state of Germany where an armed revolution is meeting an industrial strike.

(April 6, 1920)

In the plethora of presidential candidates now deafening the air with their building of personal platforms, it is very pleasant to remember that only one of them can be elected.

(April 8, 1920)

The Formula for Government Whitewash.

We must note that an Anxious Inquirer wrote Mr. Haskin about the formula for government whitewash. And while we have every respect for Mr. Haskin's ability we have a feeling that he missed something. Now if the A. I. had asked us, we would have said, as follows:

One large newspaper scandal, taken up all over the country.
Many complaints to congress.
Five months later congress appoints an investigating committee.
Investigating committee appoints subcommittees for research.
One subcommittee goes to the Panama Canal to study conditions.
Another subcommittee runs up to Atlantic City to study conditions.
Third subcommittee goes to San Francisco to study conditions.
Five months later report is handed in.
Investigating committee finds the report on its desk one day and throws it
 in waste basket.
Five months later investigating committee reports to congress:
Conditions thoroughly investigated. No report necessary.
Blame fixed on the general public.
There's your government whitewash.

(May 3, 1920)

If the new method of international politics continues we suggest an exchange of political candidates. [French premier Georges] Clemenceau would make an excellent president for us and goodness knows we could spare Mr.[Postmaster Albert] Burleson for Armenia. And Eugene V. Debs for Mexico.

(May 9, 1920)

"Stone walls," according to Eugene V. Debs, "Do not a prison make." But on the other hand we aren't convinced that they make a good White House.[3]

(May 15, 1920)

Now is the time for a good Ouija board to come to the aid of the parties.

(May 16, 1920)

Having learned that Woodrow Wilson's chief passion is for circuses, we know now why he was so anxious to be present at the peace conference.

(May 23, 1920)

It seems quite obvious after a careful perusal of the national press that a lot of editors could write better editorials about the Mexican question if they could find out a little more about what is really going on.

(May 25, 1920)

The war to make the world safe for democracy has not yet made the democrats safe from war.

(May 27, 1920)

Alice in Woodrow Land.

 "You are old, Father Woodrow" the public said
 And your rule has become very tight.
Your dictums eternally stand on their head,
"It is, for democracy, right?"

"In my youth," Father Woodrow replied to the land,
 "I feared someone would rigidly reign.
But now that it's I that is taking this stand,
Why, I do it again and again."

"You are old," said the public, "as we said before."
"And your order you give very flat.
 Yet you turned all your principles out of the door.
Pray, what is the meaning of that?"

"In my youth," said our Woodrow, with repartee deft,
 "I kept all my views very supple.
So when one wouldn't work, I had others left.
 Allow me to give you a couple."

"You are old," said the public, "And you say you're too weak
 To solve any national crisis.
Yet you're yanking Turkey around by the beak,
Forgetting our H.C.L. [high cost of living] prices."

"In my youth," said our Woodrow, "I found it was right,
 In settling a vexing discussion,

To wander afar from the scene of the Fight
And never the danger to rush on."

"You are old," said the public, "We'd hardly suppose
That your strength was as hearty as ever.
Yet you lead lots of Democrats round by the nose.
What makes you so awfully clever?"

"I have answered three questions and that is enough"
Said our Woodrow, "You're only a worm.
Do you think I don't know that your attitude's bluff?
And besides, I may want a third term."

(May 30, 1920)

There are two sound arguments against politics. The first is that they keep so many men running who were obviously built to walk and the second is that they are politics.

(June 5, 1920)

The Voice of the People.

Now that it is all over, speaking, as we have so often, politically, we can safely analyze, several political pronouncements of man, the reasoning animal, which we have heard recently. They had to do with why they were going to vote as they presumably have.

1. He was not going to vote for A because his wife did not like A's looks.
2. He was going to vote for B because for years they had had the same doctor.
3. He was not going to vote for A because he did not like the way he advertised.
4. He was going to vote for A because he spent no money on his campaign, for B in spite of the fact that he spent money on his campaign.
5. He was going to vote for C because his second cousin had been given a political appointment by C.
6. He was going to vote for D to spite his neighbor, who opposed him.

7. He was going to vote for E because E always shook hands with him on the street.
8. He was not going to vote for F because F came from a town where he had once spent the night and there was a leak in the roof of his hotel.
9. He was going to vote for G because everybody else was going to.
10. He was going to vote for H because he was not the popular candidate.

(June 9, 1920)

In spite of the late buzzing of political bees we don't notice there has been any change in the price of honey.

(June 11, 1920)

If the next war is, as has been predicted, in the air, the heads of the war, navy and postal departments are there already.

(June 16, 1920)

Probably the reason that nominating speeches are such poor things is that they have nothing to do at all with the real nominations.

Now that the Anti-Saloon League has gained prohibition, someone ought to prohibit the Anti-Saloon League.

(June 17, 1920)

Even after we have heard all about the Republican platform we can't seem to remember anything about it except that the Republican party wants to beat the Democrats. As a platform itself it would make an excellent mosquito net.

F.P.A. [columnist of the *New York Tribune*] says that more people are probably reading the Elwell case in the newspapers than ever glanced at the accounts of the recent political conventions, which proves that murder cases are always better written. We would suggest that if a few of the candidates at Chicago had been killed off for one reason or another the entire country would have been aroused from its boredom. It wasn't even a good scrap.

May the best man win.

But, we admit, it doesn't often happen that way.

(June 24, 1920)

The Democrats seem to have attributed every good thing to the present [Wilson] administration except the California climate and one-piece bathing suits.

(July 4, 1920)

Democracy for most people means an equal chance for them to get ahead of someone else.

(July 11, 1920)

Germany's idea of the [Versailles peace] treaty seems to be the same as that of the alcoholic gentleman before Prohibition, he could take it or leave it alone.

(July 17, 1920)

The photographs of both [presidential] candidates, taken before and after the nomination, show little improvement in their worried expressions.

(July 23, 1920)

Now that Attorney General Palmer has announced his intention of annihilating the coal profiteers, we may expect them to enter upon a period of unparalleled prosperity.

People have been worrying what this country will do when the oil gives out. But why worry when the profiteers are still slick and the politicians smooth.

(August 5, 1920)

Gene Debs is one candidate whose prowess on the golf links never bores us.

(August 17, 1920)

In these days of heated political controversy it is a pleasant thing to remember that someone said that causes should be judged by their merits and not by their worst advocates.

(September 14, 1920)

I cannot understand why a man is supposed to be eligible to any office if he is plain and blunt. So is a rusty hatchet.

(September 18, 1920)

The popular fear of getting another so-called scholar in the White House (since to the popular mind any man who has written a book of nonfiction is a scholar, as per W. W. [Woodrow Wilson]) may be allayed by Mr. Harding's remark about Mansfield's production of "Charles V." Charles or Henry, what does it matter. That's highbrow stuff.

(September 29, 1920)

The prohibitionists say that the liquor issue is as dead as slavery. The wet people say that liquor can be obtained anywhere. You'd think they'd both be satisfied.

(October 7, 1920)

The prohibitionists used to call whiskey "Devil's Dynamite." And yet nowadays you can't carry a quart of whiskey in a car without getting overhauled for it, while wagon loads of dynamite may wander through any city and blow up on any street corner as they please. Which goes to show whatever it goes to show.

(October 10, 1920)

While the good people are taking up the agitation against tobacco, would it be asking too much of them not to overlook the demon chewing gum? The harm it does to a pretty girl's face is almost incalculable.

(October 13, 1920)

We were awfully discouraged yesterday when we read that Harding liked sentimental novels and thought that "The Passing of the Third Floor Back" was the greatest drama ever written. We were discouraged, that is, for the national standards. But we have been reading about Brother Cox's taste in literature and now we know the worst. There is no hope. Cox says he likes any kind of book that either entertains or instructs. And both of these two, count them, both, were brought up to read nothing but "Fox's Book of Martyrs" and "The Pilgrim's Progress." Shades of Irvin Cobb, have we sunk so low?

At the same time, while we haven't asked him, and probably no one will, we are willing to bet that Eugene Debs would score over both of them.

(October 12, 1920)

The present Republican-Democrat party scrap in Miami has not proved anything very much yet except that all party politics are an old-fashioned, noisy, illogical, unnecessary nuisance. Otherwise, we have no complaint to make.

(October 19, 1920)

While we may make many shrewd criticisms of the present political campaign, at least it is only fair to say that by keeping real issues carefully in the background it has spared us the necessity of getting all worked up about it.

(October 30, 1920)

Although the world has been made safe for democracy there are many nations yet to be convinced that democracy is safe for them.

(November 20, 1920)

From the latest accounts the League of Nations would appear to be rather a bush league. Candor compels us to say that we stole this idea from a nameless exchange which didn't phrase it half so well.

The Wichita public library received a naughty new book in a recent shipment, and placed it on the call shelf before learning its contents. The

[Wichita] Eagle intimates that the library will bar it from circulation as soon as the woman who has had it out two weeks overtime brings it back.

(November 28, 1920)

The allies seem not to be agreed on many things except about the size of the [war] bills they would like the United States to pay.

(November 30, 1920)

Those Blue Law Blues.[4]

We've got the Blue Law blues,
And we're feelin' mighty—
I said mighty—
I mean, bad.
We've got the Blue Law blues.
Well, the Blue Laws ain't nothin' but the ole U.S. gone mad.

Oh, blue law Sunday,
is so awful long and—
I said long and—
I mean, tough—
Oh, the blue law Sunday is so awful long and tough,
They needn't be surprised if they make us cut up rough.

The preachers and the good folks,
Want to make us solemn—
I said solemn—
I mean, sad.
But the preachers and the good folks 'll only make us dog-gone
 mad.

We've got the Blue Law blues.
And we're gettin' peevish—
I said, peevish—
I mean, sore.
But if these narrow-eyed, long-lipped lank-jawed spinsters of
 both sexes really want to take the joy out of livin',
They'll have to do a whole lot more.

(December 5, 1920)

Now that everyone from the Pope down has endorsed Herbert Hoover's plan for saving the starving children of Europe nothing remains to be done but doing it.[5]

(December 8, 1920)

The next amendment to the Constitution should be no more amendments to the Constitution. In other words, we nominate the statute of limitations.

If all those newspapers that are arguing about the vintage of Senator Harding's word "bloviate" would kindly tell us what they think it means, they would be doing a great deal more toward making the world safe for normalcy for us.[6]

(December 10, 1920)

The Volstead Act seems to have exchanged the crime of drunkenness for the crime of murder.

(December 12, 1920)

The more one reads of the Geneva conference, popularly known as the League of Nations, the more humorous it sounds. Now comes the revelation that the little nations who went into the league arrived at Geneva with the firm intention of getting the power away from the big nations, England, France and Italy, and then insisting on disarmament. But the big three were ready for them and have not allowed them to get any power and therefore have done nothing in the way of disarmament. The only touch of humor is the fact that the United States is not represented so that it could take a high moral ground on something or other based entirely on facts supplied by one of the big powers with no ax to grind. The spectacle of the U.S. as a disinterested observer is really the only sane thing in the whole league mess, but of course prevents us from a whole columnful of humorous observation every now and then. We will bear this loss, however, as cheerfully as we can under the circumstances.

(December 17, 1920)

From now until March we can brace ourselves for a long period of discussion about the inauguration festivities in which the phrase "Jeffersonian simplicity" will be taken out of the archives, dusted off and then ignored. The real preparations for the inauguration were made when the Republicans decided not to appoint those worthy Democrats still on Wilson's appointment list. That's Jeffersonian simplicity for you.

(January 11, 1921)

Mr. Harding would be doing a greater thing for the country if he should arrange that the inaugural weather should also be a Jeffersonian simplicity.

(January 18, 1921)

Advice to the Young.
My child, Be-hold the Pol-i-tician
Devoid of all else but Am-bition.
He calls up-on the Pres-Elect
To Pay him Hon-or and Re-spect.
Ab-out his Health he oft In-quires
He'd ne-ver call it "Pull-ing Wires."
His Neck-ties are not Very Pret-ty.
He works, by Choice, with a Com-mit-tee.
My Child, Grow Up with One Con-dition.
Don't Ev-er Be a Pol-i-tician.

(February 14, 1921)

The United States is made up of two kinds of people: those who think the prohibition amendment works and those who wonder when it is going to begin.

(March 16, 1921)

If the reports from Russia as to all the revolutions and counter-revolutions are true, it would appear that Russia hates to give up its prominent position in the newspaper world to the island of Yap.[7]

If his eight years of service pretty nearly killed President Wilson, is it any wonder that the country is finding it a little slow to recuperate at the present moment?[8]

(March 19, 1921)

For 25 years no bread has been baked in Norway on Sunday, which ought to please the Blue Law people except that the reason may be that Norway then does something else with the yeast.

(March 23, 1921)

One good reason why they haven't succeeded in getting everything they want from Germany is probably because they haven't yet threatened her with prohibition.

(April 1, 1921)

It is said that if the ladies would refrain from the use of face powder for one year they would save the price of the navy bill. Curiously enough, it is always the women who are appealed to. Now no one has suggested yet that if we refrained from building so many dreadnaughts it would save the price not only of face powder, but of a good deal of baking powder biscuit for the people as well.

In fact, speaking of navies, everyone seems to be agreed that disarmament is absolutely necessary for the future of the world, but while we are waiting for someone else to start we might as well be turning out a few more battleships.

(April 2, 1921)

The new Polish constitution makes religion free. Considering the present state of Europe we can't help expecting that everything else will be cash.

(April 13, 1921)

What this country really needs is a little legislation that will make people squeeze toothpaste from the end of the tube instead of the middle.

(April 14, 1921)

Once in a while we can't help feeling that it is time for us to take our attention off art and literature in order to settle a few important political questions. We don't like to do it often because the older we grow the more we realize that politics are less political when let alone. One day off a month should be ample time for any sensible person to make up his mind about these things; as for instance—

Considering that the battleships which Mr. [Secretary of State Charles Evans] Hughes and everyone are so excited about scrapping, have been generally considered to be obsolete, anyway, somehow we can't help wondering what the excitement is all about.

The more you see of the arguments between nations the more you realize, if you are the realizing kind, that they are always arguments about economic boundaries. That is, about tariffs. That is the chief difficulty between France and Germany. That is the Japanese question. That is the Chinese problem, the Silesian[9] question hung upon it. The Balkans are constantly torn by it. The one universal necessity for industrial stability is free access to markets. Put a tariff between the United States and Canada and we would have war in two years. Put a tariff between Florida and Alabama and we would have one in a year. Put a tariff between Dade County and Broward County and you'll fight tomorrow.

(November 30, 1921)

The question has been asked whether the disarmament movement, which apparently began with the limitation of the old time schooners, will extend also to California naval oranges?

(December 18, 1921)

It is a curious thing, but a true one, that deep in all our hearts we suspect the professional politician. I think that is why we really suspect all con-

gressmen and senators, because we know that not one of them has reached Washington without a certain amount of log-rolling. And a certain amount of log-rolling in any man's life makes him a second-rate man. Can't help it. Therefore, we suspect politicians and the practices of politicians, because we know that, as they have not reached their present position disinterestedly, so their lawmaking cannot be wholly disinterested. We know that personal values, not direct personal aggrandizement, lie behind their decisions, whether for improvements in their own bailiwicks or dictums about disarmament. If they were first-rate men, instead of second-rate men, we would neither have the spectacle of continuous political inconsistency in high places nor the suspicion with which we are accustomed to regard them. To take politics out of government is not enough. In fact, it is not possible. It must be the second-rate man who is taken out of government, since, by his very second-rateness, he has proved that he is unfit to govern himself. But this is the evil of democracy, which democracy has not yet tried to overcome.

(December 30, 1921)

The W.C.T.U. [Women's Christian Temperance Union] has discovered a way of making prohibition work. They have devised a beautiful little banner with one star in the center, which will be hung on the door of all houses where no drop of liquor is ever to be found. The caption of a photograph we have recently seen says, "The policeman will not worry about your house when he sees this flag in the window." It is said there is quite a rush on the part of prominent bootleggers to secure flags.

(January 24, 1922)

From a Journalist's Day Book.

Monday, September 25.

Here we go, according to the newspapers, warming up the political questions, so that we'll all get excited enough by fall to go and vote. And here we go again, the same old round of political incrimination and recrimination, with the party in power wanting to stay in and the party out of power

wanting to get in. The Republicans have made just about the same mess of things that the Democrats did awhile ago, yet because the Democrats are out of power they can speak virtuously, while the Republicans can only point with pride to the achievements of their career and avoid all reference to the real achievements, which are a lot of fool legislation, a high tariff that comes the nearest to being criminal of anything in the whole history of tariffs, and the development of the bureaucracy at Washington which the war began and which the Republicans, far from breaking up, augmented. So that today in Washington there are now more governmental employees than there were during the war and so that a bonus was recently voted to them, on the same basis as the recently repudiated soldier bonus, with no publicity whatsoever. But the trouble is that if the Democrats do get in they won't do much to do away with existing evils. They only create their own brand. However, if they do get the tariff repealed they will have achieved something and will have employed a real issue for the first time in many years. Of course, the fact of the matter is that you can't tell a Democrat from a Republican nowadays and neither party has any policies of any sort. That is the why of the fool legislation. Neither party is strong enough to be a check on the other. It looks like a transition stage for the parties and as if others might result. But the discouraging thing about politics is that it taints everything before long. The older I get the more opposed I get to political action of any kind. If the people only realized it, they have a power, in their own public opinion, in the force of their ideas, which will accomplish a thousand times more than politics ever will. Perhaps they are realizing that, and perhaps we are outgrowing this violent political activity. Let's hope so. It will give us a chance to get down to business and do a little of our own work. "The least possible government and the greatest possible freedom of the people." Whoever said it was right.

"The per capita wealth of the United States increased 46 cents during the month of August"—Press Dispatch.

But there is no need to worry. The tariff will take care of the surplus.

(October 2, 1922)

We see by the papers that some of the Democrats are in, and some of the Republicans are out. This is the way we said it would be, and we are willing

to bet right now that until this country gets a real pair of parties, with real issues, in place of these two figureheads, that all elections will always go this way. The ones that are on the outside hurling mud will get in and the ones on the inside, trying to cover up their takings, will get out. The system of misgovernment under each will be slightly different, but the country will wag on just about as usual. We are willing to let this statement stand for any number of elections, until such time as everybody recognizes that the greatness of the Democrats and the Republicans, as valuable parties, passed away long since.

We understand that you pronounce "Fascisti" as if it were "Fash-isti." It was high time we ourselves were learning to say it, because something tells us that Italy is due for such high old times, with roaring sentimentalists who believe in force and imperialism in the saddle, that we had better learn to pronounce it before it is too late.

Something tells us that all this conversation of Mr. Secretary Weeks on the follies of unpreparedness would indicate that those at Washington who control our foreign policy are thinking of annexing a few more islands. If preparedness be the price of imperialism, apparently we are going to be made to like to pay for it.

Up in Raleigh [North Carolina] they are beginning to conclude that what this country needs is a good, inexpensive tar-and-feather remover.

(November 10, 1922)

The worst thing we can think of to worry about is that the new stamp just issued for the islands of St. Christopher and Nevis, in the West Indies, shows Christopher Columbus discovering the new world with a spy-glass, and the spy-glass wasn't even invented until a hundred years after Columbus died.

(November 11, 1922)

When the colonies were ready to become the United States of America they drew up that remarkable document which we sometimes forget, which we know as the Declaration of Independence. That document stated that

America was to be founded on the equal chance to "life, to liberty and to the pursuit of happiness." It has been a long time since that document was written and it has been forgotten time and time again that that statement, and that statement only, is the justification, the explanation, and the whole meaning of America. If we have failed as a nation it is because we have forgotten it. But down here in South Florida we believe that it is not too late to make that come true.

(December 29, 1922)

Politics are not much in our line and we are not ever very intelligent about the value of the opinion of some of the leading characters in our great national indoor sport. But it strikes us that Senator [William E.] Borah said a good thing recently, which shows an unusual amount of hard common sense, whatever his usual habit in the matter of common sense may be. He said it would be a better thing for the country if we stopped trying to build up bureaus in Washington and started building communities at home. The fine meaning of that remark you will not appreciate unless you know what a community is. Because obviously Mr. Borah could not have meant simply a geographical locality, or even a political place. What he undoubtedly meant was that a community is something which must be built up in a place, out of the people in it. It is a certain purpose in common, it is a certain likemindedness, which the war taught us that we must have, if we are ever to do anything together intelligent. We need communities, rather than just towns full of unrelated, disassociated people. Until any place, and the people in it, really becomes a community, it will never get very far, and its people will never live very interesting or valuable lives. More than bureaus in Washington, more, we venture to add to the senator's statement, more even than politics, we must set ourselves to the building of communities, rather than just places. The more a place is a real community, where the citizens have a pleasant and stimulating life in common, where there is an interchange of friendliness, where they put the advancement of the whole before their individual gains, the more truly American it will be, the more truly it will bring to the country at large what it must have. It is a greater work, according to Mr. Borah, if we may be permitted to continue to interpret him, to get a city to work together for one big splendid thing, in which they can sink their petty spites, their neighborhood jealousness,

their feuds, than to go to Washington and found a bureau which will try to produce results for a town from the outside, paternalistically and of necessity superficially. The work of bureaus in Washington, by which service of experts is given to the community, after the community is established, is invaluable, but the community must come first. I wonder how much of a real community Miami is? It has very much and very genuine spirit for its progress. But is it a well-knit community as a whole? That would be an interesting question to try to answer, wouldn't it?

(March 29, 1923)

Of course, as the South's Only [the *Miami Herald*] insists, Mr. Harding is our president and all that, but we note where he recently departed from his safe course of not stating too hard and fast opinions about things and came right out in meeting and declared rashly to the mayor of Hartford that Shakespeare's works constitute part of the magnificent joint heritage of the British and American peoples.

(May 1, 1923)

To be satisfied with mediocrity is surely a grave charge about any nation. It is a charge which one can make about the voting classes of most countries, nowadays. And it is worse than a serious situation. It is an idiotically stupid one.

(May 28, 1923)

Nobody has yet started a movement to award a prize to the members of the late Florida legislature for their earnest and efficient work in not passing all the bills that were brought to them to pass. More bills than ever before were brought, it is said, and fewer were passed. And while we think they were absolutely wrong in not passing that one which would have limited the sale of submerged lands in Biscayne Bay, still the tendency is an admirable one. If you count up the number of legislators throughout the country and the number of laws they pass in a session, and add that to congress, you will discover that we are the most lavishly governed people in the world. We have so many laws that no ordinary citizen can possibly know all of them,

and we seem to have a mad passion for making more. We don't seem to take into account the relation of this passion to the high tax rate, but there is something somewhere. In Switzerland once, it seems, a condition like this arose, and the people called a commission who chose something like 20,000 laws out of the lot as a permanent code and threw the rest overboard. And you know what people say about the government of Switzerland.

(June 9, 1923)

⤙4⤚ Woman

Faithful readers of The Galley would have known that "MSD" had been a suffragist and that she had outspoken views on the subject of men and women. Her usual style was to poke fun, often deploying one-line quips, at male-female tradition and at men who had low opinions of women.

After her marriage to Kenneth, Douglas could have easily grown bitter toward men. It is revealing of her character that she did not. She walked away from her marriage regretting not male companionship but her judgment in choosing and staying with Kenneth. She described it as "an impossible, not unrewarding marriage," and embraced it as a learning experience.[1] Eight years after her divorce, she reflected on that lesson in her diary: "Marriage as a goal is passive, unless coincidentally with the idea of marriage a woman has constructively developed her personality in such a fashion as to be a powerful directing force in the life of the man she marries."[2] Douglas herself never remarried, but she still enjoyed male friendships. Even as she criticized the overbearing male personality, she made a point of recognizing men of intelligence and principle.

Douglas also appreciated the chivalrous male; yet she maintained a clear idea of where women belonged in society—on the same footing as men. Women exercised the vote in a national election for the first time in 1920, the year that Douglas introduced her column, but equal footing was far from a reality. She did not decry the role of women in the home, only the idea of women being confined to the home within the social prescription of separate spheres for the sexes. First as a suffragist then as a newspaper writer, she had been among an early group of women in modern Florida to pierce the public sphere made virtually exclusive to men. Douglas applauded women who pursued a career in male-dominated professions, such as science and medicine, and even after she stopped voting, she en-

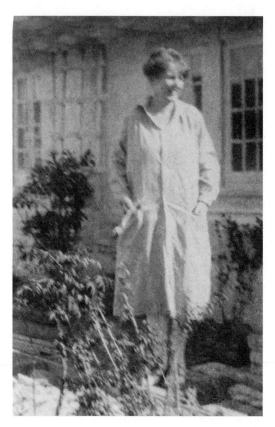

In the yard of her Coconut Grove home, 1920s. After her failed marriage and departure for Florida in 1915 Douglas preferred independence and the rewards of a writing career to the entanglement of a relationship. Courtesy of Florida State Archives.

couraged women to assert themselves in the political process. The politically active woman, she believed, had much to contribute toward the improvement of society. In Douglas's opinion, a male-dominated society was flawed. Working alone, men were not sensitive enough to the needs of the nation and its citizens to make informed decisions concerning the welfare of either. Women brought from their own experiences and socialization a fresh perspective to the public sphere of politics. Opening up the political process could potentially double the mind power behind it and broaden the flow of values and ideas. The only cost was an affordable one, in Douglas's opinion, the breakup of a male-monopolized world.

In the following passages, Douglas discusses women's issues in the context of politics, voting, marriage, divorce, fashion, and male-female relationships. She even takes an occasional stab at women themselves.

When we vote a man into office, we generally vote ourselves or some other people into prison or temple, so Mr. Voter, will you please vote for the peaceable women who are peacemakers of the world, and were never known to make prisons nor to declare war, nor to fight battles. Just so long as the world votes for he peace they will have war, and as soon as they vote and elect she peace, they will have peace, then they can come rejoicing forever in the shes.

(March 27, 1920)

There are probably more biting epigrams on the variability of women than on similar characteristics of men because the Mrs. is generally too busy washing dishes to write 'em out and send 'em in.

(April 22, 1920)

When a woman marries, her ideal becomes the man she thought her husband was before she married him.

When a man marries, his ideal becomes the woman he knows his wife will never be.

(May 1, 1920)

Suffrage may have permitted women to become candidates for office but it is the high cost of millinery that is keeping their hats out of the ring.

(May 5, 1920)

All women may be divided into two classes, those who powder their noses and those who object to cigar ashes on the carpet.

(June 2, 1920)

The Confessions of the Galley Slave.

It is a very amusing thing to hear men talk about what women will do in politics. No matter or not they are for suffrage, they unite in agreeing that women will choose their candidate, presumably masculine, solely on account of their looks. This is counted a humorous thing by men. And yet a little eavesdropping on later conversation shows us that men always judge women by their looks, whether as candidates for political or domestic offices. And that forces us to the conclusion that one sex judges the other sex by its looks, no matter which sex it is.

And that is not, after all, funny, but rather sensible. Men forget that women have very little basis for judging men as they do, because their relations with men are not at all the same. Women, who criticize men for marrying for looks and not for character, do not realize what little other basis men have for judging women's character. It is a safe bet that men would vote for the best-looking candidate just as women will have their votes much influenced by the appearance of the masculine candidate. Of the two, perhaps women would have a little advantage since women's shrewdness in judging has had to be a little more carefully cultivated.

The effect on politics may be a general improvement in the appearance of both if one can take a chance on making so general a statement. The woman candidate will more and more be the good looking, well set up, well groomed, type of woman, because she will have to be. And the effect of an audience of women votes may mean that the masculine candidate will have to care a little bit more about trimming his hair and cleaning his teeth, about getting sufficient exercise to reduce his extra embonpoint, and putting more attention on his own muscles and general set up.

We may not have any better politics on this account, but we will certainly have a better looking lot of office holders. Which would be no great tragedy.

(June 4, 1920)

Concerning Man's Favorite Topic.
Woman, if what the papers say,
 About your character is true,
A most amazing paradox
 Are you.

For years they rallied about your skirts
 Too short, too long, too wide, too antic.
You smile, Why don't the scolders drive
 You frantic?

And while they scold you for your dress
 They chide because you cannot reason
They say your sense of humor's bad
 At any season.

They say you are the spendthrift sex,
 They say you pinch the hide off nickels,
They call you stubborn as an ox,
 yet fickle.

Since twenty decades poets chant
 Your coldness, moan the way they've doted.
We learn emotion rules the way
 You've voted.

They say you're nothing but a child,
 Playing with ribbons, foolish toys,
They say a mother's heart should guide
 The boys.

A toy, a playmate, mother, friend,
 A light o' love, a doubtful blessing,
Woman, you're wise, I think, to keep
 Them guessing.

(June 11, 1920)

Now that women smoke in New York cars and Boston has smoking rooms for ladies, the Anti-Cigarette League would succeed in making me give up the coffin-nail if it called the habit "womanish."

It is not always vanity that makes a woman stare into the mirror. Sometimes she does it to assure herself that it is as bad as she feared.

At the same time men do not always gaze into a mirror only to see that their ties are on straight.

At the same time vanity like morals is chiefly a question of geography.
(July 24, 1920)

We are beginning to think that the people who, in this late day, insist on saying that woman's place is in the home, must be housing profiteers.
(July 10, 1920)

It is a curious thing that the man who mourns that woman is losing her aura of mystery complains that he can't understand her.
(July 11, 1920)

The Society for Upholding the Sanctity of Marriage is going to have an amendment to the constitution prohibiting divorce. It would be a much wiser thing to get an amendment prohibiting frocks that button in the back, ashes on the carpet, snoring, bills for millinery and all-night poker games.
(July 13, 1920)

Shoes for the fall are to be prettier and higher. But our opinion of the shoe manufacturers will be uglier and lower.
(July 23, 1920)

People are now complaining that women smoke at the races whose grand-mothers were modestly content to smoke in the chimney corner.
(July 27, 1920)

"One Third Off on Bathing Suits" says an adv. In a Washington paper. Wonder which third?

There are some men who can obey orders and then again there are some who probably never will get married.
(August 8, 1920)

The man wanted the room papered blue; the wife wanted it papered pink; so they compromised on pink.

(August 9, 1920)

Sea bathing was not really indulged in much by the masculine sex until after the Civil War. And in the middle '70s the first daring women ventured up to the ankles in the briny, clothed in long striped trousers under a very full skirt, long sleeved waists and huge hats tied down securely under the chin. Those were in the days when it was not yet decided that women had any minds at all and in some parts of the country it was still doubtful that they had souls. Children were a result of a divine dispensation and the human body was something which everyone had but which everyone was a little ashamed of.

After that, the deluge. The scandalous creatures no sooner got people accustomed to that costume, than they shortened it and went in deeper. Your scribe can remember the days of the full serge bloomers, the full braided skirt and waist with the flapping sailor collar, the heavy stockings, the e—yes, they did too, they wore them in swimming and they were the wasp waist kind at that. And no one called that immoral.

Then some bold women actually dared to try swimming, real swimming. And they not only liked it, but it was immensely good for them. It toughened the waist muscles, made flabby by years of pinching. It toughened the leg muscles so that they could not only swim but walk. It made them into real upstanding human women, fit to be thinking creatures and good mothers of good strong babies. Which, when you consider it, is a dreadfully immoral thing to be.

So they shortened the bathing suit and tightened it and cut the skirt off until it was just as sensible as the men's. And clad in one of those things, you could really tell whether a girl was the sort of girl whose children would be an asset to the community or not.

So of course, there was bound to be a lot of opposition. Because the women who couldn't wear a proper swimming suit because they wouldn't dare to would immediately call the other kind bold and designing hussies. They always do. Or they would be older women who had not brought up

their daughters so that they could be trusted by themselves and who were therefore naturally nervous. Or they were those to whom certain things seemed immoral for curious personal reasons of their own. Just as the committees of the vice commission never agree on the immoralities of books they are suppressing, for the reason that each individual of this type has a pet particular immorality.

(August 18, 1920)

If—For the Women Voters.

If you can keep your vote when all about you
 Are throwing theirs away on this and that;
If you can think with politics about you,
 Of major issues that are plain and flat;
If you can see your way through horrid speeches
 And never lose your head on flowery ways—
Then you can vote as well as who wear breeches.
 And you can vote so that the voting pays.
If you can walk through crowds that shout in passion,
 And never leave your reasoning behind;
If you can think, when feeling is the fashion,
 And never trust to luck or go it blind;
If you can keep the welfare of the nation
 Above the gain or glory of a few—
You'll make the ballot yet a decoration
 Worthy a voter, and a women, too.

(August 20, 1920)

Perhaps the people who believed that woman's place is the home have changed their minds because of the housing shortage.

An esteemed contemporary remarked some time ago that woman will vote as she rocks the cradle, for the best interests of her child. All those mothers who are in favor of rocking cradles for children, please hold up their right hands. All those who own cradles with rockers, hold up the left hand.

(August 25, 1920)

How the women will vote, what they will do in politics, are questions which even the women are being interested in these days. All the old anti-suffrage statements and arguments are hanging around the corner ready to pounce on the first unfortunate woman who casts her ballot. The "woman's place is in the home" adherents will gather little lists of statistics to show how right they were and the "politics are (or do you say is?) too rotten for them" believers will have their little proofs, too. They based their arguments on their own conception of women, derived, possibly, from their attitude toward their mothers. According to the antis women were either angels or lights o' love or goddesses or underdeveloped species of the race of which man is the fine and supreme flower. You could easily determine a man's argument against suffrage by his mental concept of women in general.

Of course the first thing that the woman voter realizes, or will realize, is that having gained the ballot she is under the same necessity as the man to make up her mind what she wants to do with it. And as the men folks this year are really very much at sea, with reason, we think, so the woman voter will find herself in the same situation. That is, of course, unless she has prejudices, as men have, about the eternal sanctity of the Democrats or the divine right of Republicanism.

But we have a sneaking suspicion that the large mass of women voters, whether they wanted the ballot or not, whether they are glad to vote or do it reluctantly only as their duty, will use that certain shrewdness and calm logic that any wife and mother uses, confronted with the daily problem of Man and his platform.

Mr. Harding, for example, says that this country should return as soon as possible to a condition of normalcy.

In the home, how is this sort of thing received?

Mr. Voter, expandingly: "Mary, we should make up our minds from now on to be extremely careful not to get sick, doctor's bills are so expensive."

Mary: "Yes, dear."

Next Morning.

Mary: "John, it looks like rain. Don't you think you better wear your rubbers?"

John: "Oh, I dunno. You women are always afraid of rain. That's only a fair weather cloud."

Mary: "Yes, dear. But you know you said yourself that we should be more careful about the doctor's bills. Your rubbers are just behind the door."

John: "Oh, I don't want to bother with my rubbers. That's just like you women. Think I'm going to get sick just because I didn't wear my rubbers!"

Mary: "You have those dreadful colds, dear. It won't take you a minute to put your rubbers on and if it should rain—"

John: Oh, all right, all right. You can't argue with a woman. I'll wear 'em just to keep you quiet, but it won't rain." Slams the door.

Rains all day. Supper.

John: "By George, it was a good thing I thought to leave my umbrella at the office the other day. I would have been soaked. Pays to have a little foresight."

Mary: "Yes, dear."

There is the perfect picture of the woman politician.

Man proposes. Woman disposes.

The country needs that sort of disposition.

(September 1, 1920)

It is now several days since the women have had the vote, and while we have spent some time in anxious observation we have yet failed to note the disintegration of the home and the defeminizing of the Lady of Our House.

(September 4, 1920)

The United States, according to the masculine pessimists, may be too highly feminized for any pleasure. But the women of Rockville Center, L.I., voted for Sunday baseball with a total of 619 out of 872. Can it be possible that the women folks are tired of that bleak Sunday afternoon feeling when the man of the house alternately dozes and grouches, proving himself very unamusing company indeed, and welcomes the chance of

having him safely out of the way, venting all his primitive instincts on the umpire of the ball game?

(September 11, 1920)

Perfect lady's problem of conduct: A woman, bitterly opposed to equal suffrage, because women "have no business mingling in politics," has been importuned to vote for the re-election of a certain senator who opposed suffrage for the same reason. Her soul revolts at the thought of entering the polls, but her sense of honor demands that she vote to reward the senatorial champion of her convictions, even though his fight was unsuccessful. What should she do?

(September 14, 1920)

Women make the mistake of judging a man by what he says, not by what he does.

Men make the mistake of judging a woman by how she looks, not by where she looks.

Whenever a woman makes a fool of a man you can be sure that he supplied her with excellent raw material.

(October 1, 1920)

You can get a woman to tell her age. You can induce her to tell you how much henna she had in her last shampoo. She can be cajoled into showing you her photograph at fourteen. But no woman worthy of the name will admit that she remained a spinster because she couldn't help it.

At the same time, the man who, at the age of 25, did not have his pick of sweethearts simply has never existed at all, anywhere.

(October 12, 1920)

A woman spends half of her life practicing the arts that will attract a husband and then puts in the other half forgetting them in order to make him comfortable.

A woman's idea of a happy marriage is the perpetual repetition of the first four days after their engagement was announced.

A man's idea of a happy marriage is something as inconspicuous as his oldest hat, as well fitting as his smoking jacket and as full of constant interest as a variety show.

These two ideas are two of the best reasons why many people do not think marriage is a success.

(October 23, 1920)

Now that the women have voted we can't help hoping that they will stop worrying about their rights long enough to put a few in practice.

(November 5, 1920)

Perhaps because it is a woman's privilege to change her mind she often gets a better one than the men who have to keep on with the old one after it's practically worn to rags.

(November 11, 1920)

Even the most ardent suffragist cannot deny that in gaining the ballot women have lost their most priceless feminine prerogative—that of blaming the men for the whole works.

(November 17, 1920)

The men who object to taking the "obey" out of the marriage ceremony are generally those who object to taking the ashes out of the fireplace on a cold morning.

(November 29, 1920)

The man who says that he understands women is the man who believes that all women are light-minded and he is the electricity.

(November 30, 1920)

If women have ever had the feeling that politics was (or do you say were?) a dark and masculine mystery, they ought to hear the conversation of a lot of newspaper men who have been with the political game since the beginnings. They would learn from them that all politicians are as skittish as women are reputed to be, as difficult to stick to a point they have made, as timid, as moody, as full of personality and lights and shadows and varyings and veerings, as the most feminine of feminine creatures have been reported to be since Eve.

(February 3, 1923)

And you know not a single Florida legislator has announced that he will introduce a bill prohibiting high heels for women? Women vote now, you know.

(March 16, 1921)

The Watch in the Masculine.
(The recently dissolved Woman's Party have announced that they will maintain a Watch Tower day and night for purpose of keeping an eye on the passage of bills in which they are interested—News Item.)

It may be soon forgotten
When the senate was so rotten.
And the house could go rampaging on a lark.
For the martial-handed females
Who grabbed off the vote from he-males
Are going to see that congress toes the mark.
Stern spinsters will glower
From the Woman's Own Watch Tower
To see that matrimony bills are passed,
While a flying squad of flappers,
Expert hunters and man-trappers,
Will lash unruly members to the mast.

Can't you see the senate smirking
When they really should be working

When the watchers wear their smartest hats and smiles?
Can't you hear the speeches thicken
When some lobbying young chicken
From the Watch Tower devastates them with her wiles?

Then the senate, as diversion,
Will be asked on an excursion
To the Tower for a genial cup of tea.
Where, after that mild jorum,
If they find they have a quorum,
They can polish off some bills informally.

In fact, I think no hobby
Could be nicer than this lobby,
With the women watching daily from the steeple.
But I wonder if all men did
What these workers have intended,
 What would happen to the wishes of the people?

(May 12, 1921)

Another Song of Divorce.

You made me what I am today
 But I'm not satisfied.
I'm going home to Ma until
 My case in court is tried.
And then I hope they'll make you pay
 When I get my decree.
You made me what I am today.
 A happy divorcee.

(March 26, 1921)

The really latest idea for smart brides is to give them book showers. At the time of going to press we have not heard what books are being considered the best showerers but after a little careful thought we have decided that any such deluge should be a complete washout unless it contained the

following: "Travels With a Donkey," Masefield's "Enslaved," Charles Reade's "It's Never Too Late to Mend," Bernard Shaw's "You Never Can Tell," Wells's "The War of the Worlds," and Darwin's "The Descent of Man." That ought to cover the subject.

(June 14, 1921)

A man who writes sometimes for the South's Only [the *Miami Herald*] a while ago said that a woman asked him why [it was] that men generally preferred to talk to men rather than women. He said it was because women didn't give the men a chance to talk and they were too polite to interrupt. Now that is a serious charge, if true, and we suspect that it is. It sounds familiar, somehow. It may be that women have bad manners toward men, after complaining all these years that American men are lacking in gallantry. In fact, we are pretty sure of it. But even more, we should say, the reason that men and women do not talk more to each other in groups is because men and women as a rule do not choose to talk about the same things in the same way. What women say is generally interesting to women, and not to men. What men say seems to interest other men more than it does women. Which goes to prove that the spheres of men and women, the course and direction of their thoughts, in spite of all the conversation about modernity, are not the same. Women like to retail personal characteristics, men like to tell anecdotes. When women argue, they become extremely vehement from the personal point of view; they are likely to become vindictive beyond reason. Men rather resent this, because they like to argue from generalities and principles, except where their personal profit is concerned. Neither is more consistent than the other, necessarily, but each thinks the other is illogical. Men argue from the abstract to the particular, women from the particular to the abstract. They have little actual mental contact because their ordinary spheres are so different unless their work happens to coincide. Women think men should be satisfied to hear them talk; men are silent and get grumpy when asked to talk when they don't want to. Either is most interesting when talking about something of which he or she has actual knowledge. Since man's practical knowledge is of necessity of wider range than woman's, it is more likely that you will hear good talk among men than among women, as an average. Man has the advantage because he has been trained to be more impersonal. The thing

which is called woman's instinct is an initial shrewdness, which is generally right, often applied wrongly, for the lack of a wide background of experience. When men and women argue impersonally, with the same definition of terms and with an equal array of facts, then there will be no questions as to which is the most interesting to listen to. Then both will have something to say. Until then, groups are likely to separate to follow their own personal tastes in conversation, which are naturally, as we are excepting flirtations, with their own sex.

(December 15, 1921)

It is a funny thing, but did you ever stop to wonder what has become of the old maid? She isn't any more. As a type she is as extinct as the well-known dodo, however extinct that is. She used to be the repressed odd woman, who, for some reason or other, didn't get married, and she lived with her brother or her sister and did the family darning and was the one to get slighted when anyone had to and was a second mother to the children without getting much of the glory. Well, where is she today? The ones that might have been her—might have been her, that sounds funny, doesn't it?—might have been she—well, anyway, the ones who might have been old maids are out writing columns in newspapers or running farms or being lawyers or painting pictures or doing—well, frankly, doing a lot of awfully interesting things and having a great time at it. Those must have been dreadful days, mustn't they, when woman's place was the home, whether they had any or not? I'm willing to bet that more women have homes than ever used to since they have done what the anti-suffragists used to call "deserted the home." Goodness, how long ago that seems and now whoever says anything about suffragists or antis now? We were one once, come to think of it, and yet look what we think of both parties today. Not fit even to put in a newspaper column. And so the old maid has gone for good and there's nobody to send comic valentines to. So much for the value of being an independent economic unit.

(October 1, 1922)

Virginia got back from New York with longer skirts. But not too long. And the word for winter is linen for us. But I'm betting a dollar to a plugged

nickel that they'll be short again next spring. How you gonna keep 'em down on the farm after they've seen Paree?

(October 2, 1922)

There was the time in France when another girl and I were going to Lake Geneva to meet ninety Belgian children and take them back home. Going was a hard trip, for we had to change cars constantly, at Lyons and at Bourg-en-Bresse and various other places. And at Bourg-en-Bresse we arrived at nine o'clock at night to take a train out at 3 o'clock. We piled off the train in our wrinkled uniforms, our musette bags over our shoulders, and reconnoitered. The station platform was dark and empty except for one infinitely dear figure at the end, a tall, lanky American M.P. We fell on his neck, of course, and asked him about hotels. There was one near the station, but he, assuming the paternal manner of all the A.E.F. [American Expeditionary Force], said he couldn't possibly let us go to that one. But if we would wait ten minutes until he was relieved he would take us to another. So we did and he did, walking down endless black streets, past a horrible-looking insane asylum, but arriving in due course at the Hotel de l'Europe, of sacred memory. Henry James says somewhere that is the most delightful hotel in France and we believed it. There was a motherly woman at the desk and huge puffy beds and hot water in cans and that was about the last we knew until the porter knocked us up at 2 a.m., in the dark, and we stumbled up to hot chocolate and fresh petit pains. But down in the lobby, fast asleep, who should we discover but that blessed boy. He had come to take us to the station. He said he hadn't liked the idea of our going through those streets alone. And he insisted on carrying our musettes. That was the sort of thing that made you feel that every last doughboy, no matter how tough or awkward or embittered, no matter how many swear words he couldn't help using, was your long-lost elder brother. Goodness, how fine they were. Then there was a morning on the Italian border—

(October 23, 1922)

The principles of evolution and the fine health of the scientific spirit, applied to human relations, are the first factors in this renascence, the growth toward democracy. Mr. [Havelock] Ellis does not say [in *The New Spirit*]

that we have as yet achieved democracy. He recognizes, as we are all begin-
ning to recognize, that that is an ideal to be struggled for. But we have been
growing a little more democratic. How does Mr. Ellis find that out? He
believes the second factor of renascence is the great wave of emancipation
for women which has been sweeping the world. Women are the new ele-
ment. "It is no wonder," he says, "that many worthy people look with dread
upon the slow invasion by women of all the concerns of life—which are,
after all, as much their concerns as any one's—as nothing less than a new
irruption of barbarians. These good people are unquestionably right. The
development of women means a re-invigoration as complete as any
brought by barbarians to an effete and degenerating civilization. When we
turn to those early societies, which are as lamps to us in our social progress,
we find that the arts of life are in the possession of women. Therefore, when
the torch of science is placed in the hands of women, we must expect them
to use it as a guide with audacious simplicity and directness because of
those instincts for practical life which they have inherited."

The influence of science, the influence of women, are both on their way
to be fulfilled more completely. The influence of democracy is not yet. But
by the new spirit which is already abroad in the world it is on a better road.
"If democracy means a state in which every man shall be a freeman, neither
in economic nor intellectual nor normal subjection, two processes at least
are needed to render democracy possible—on the one hand, a large and
many-sided education; on the other, the reasonable organization of life."
(November 23, 1922)

The man who ventures to say nowadays that all that women are fit for is to
pull a plow, or to wash dishes only, has to be able to stand more kidding
than is exactly human. It is getting a little bit late in the day for men to
object that women are getting outside their proper sphere. Nobody knows
yet what is either man's or woman's proper sphere, or how they are to find
it. There is no way of going, but to go forward, my masters.

It really is funny, when you come to think of it, the amount of talk and
speculation and writing which has been done by men on the subject of
women since man became the sort of animal which could express himself.
You read books written by men on the subject of women, of what women

think, of how women act and react, just as if this other sex were a different race entirely, a race of queer, half mad, wholly incomprehensible beings. Of course the world is gradually getting over that stage, partly because [women] speak for themselves. But in every newspaper gust of excitement you read the same old atavistic fear, perhaps, of the unknown. Even now, the question of whether or not a woman has a soul is discussed solemnly by important doctors and argued in many a pulpit. To add to this occasional gust of medievalism, men accuse women of not having a sense of humor . . .

(December 2, 1922)

The bill of rights of the woman's party strikes us rather funny. Somehow, in spite of the fact that we once, right in our own Tallahassee, lobbied for woman's suffrage and had our best dress endangered by the lavish expectorations of our representative's pet spittoon we sat near, in spite of the fact that it irritates us when men make fun of women's clothes as slaves to convention, and all that sort of thing, somehow the idea of the women's party thinking that it would be able to remove all inequalities between men and women by an Act of Congress appeals to us immensely as material for a pseudo-funny column. We stopped voting suddenly a while ago, after we had gone through all the agony to get the vote, chiefly because we wanted time to decide how important politics really are. And we may any minute decide to stop worrying about men's and women's inequalities for the reason that we have not noticed any recently. We have noticed men taking their hats off to us in elevators and we have rather liked it, but not knowing whether it was up to us to say, "Thanks, awfully," or smile or bow or what. We have noticed that men open doors for women and we have rather liked that, too. But as to more inequalities that exist between individuals anyway, whether of the opposite sex or not, we really have been too busy to reconnoiter. Personally, we believe in two things, the individual and the community, and we do not see how sex really matters. If people would only stop worrying one way or the other about sex, and let us forget it a little, it would be a great comfort. What with the prudists who think it is immoral and the radicals who think it is essential, the people who think it is altogether unimportant haven't much chance. We strongly believe, however, that these last are the people who accomplish things.

(December 27, 1922)

For Women Only.

Although a minor bard am I
And humble quite before my betters,
Its oft that risibility
Conquers my awe for Them of Letters.
Some weighty male, some poet wight
Who waxes eloquent and tender
About the dim, mysterious light
With which he views the female gender.
"O woman," so he writes, indeed,
Who likes to think them soft and stupid.
O beauteous woman—that's his creed.
The slaves, he feels, of Mister Cupid.
The lovely little fluttering things,
So fragile, such celestial flowers.
"This world's too tough for you," he sings
And twirls a pallid lute for hours.
While all around him womankind
Are silent, waiting the occasion.
Amused to mark his type of mind
Is common to the male persuasion.
Strong, silent women, quick and grim,
Alert to seize, to snatch, to batter.
You bet, they don't sing hymns to him.
They march upon the things that matter.
And if he thinks they have no brains
because their hands are white and clinging,
Let him continue his refrains.
Great goodness, girls, let's keep him singing.

(March 3, 1923)

It is interesting to note, these years since suffrage was given women, just
what has happened to the mind of the woman as citizen. So many miracu-
lous and so many dreadful things were promised for it, that it hardly seems
possible that we can all be as calm as we seem to be. As far as it appears in
Florida, nothing much has happened, because for the most part women

have lined up with the parties and thrown their votes in the usual manner. But gradually a little difference may be discerned, not so much in the matter of voting but in the measures sponsored by women for the legislature. And this thing seems to be true. Men are chiefly interested in the material improvement of their parts of the state, naturally, since for the most part they are the breadwinners. They are interested in roads, bridges, deeper harbors, no-fence laws, and such excellent measures, all related in some way to their earning capacities. Now the women voters are interested in these things also, but when they sponsor especially a bill in legislature you may notice that it is not material improvements which they desire for the state or their locality. The thing that interests them is the welfare and advancement of people. That is, it is a generally recognized fact that women's genius lies especially along the lines of social organization, and of course by social I do not mean the pink teas and dinner parties of so-called society. Women are concerned with the welfare of people, of children, primarily, and of adults also. That is why we are finding the first movement for a public welfare department as a state institution receiving the support and recognition first of women. Of course men are recognizing it also, but not quite so wholeheartedly. We are not forgetting for a moment that it was the Kiwanis club of Miami which first directed the attention of the people here to the subject of county organization for child welfare. But the women as a whole recognized the need of that sort of thing first. In social matters also, women are still the conservers of life, more than the creators of material welfare. I think that will be remarked more and more and I am not at all sure that that is not a natural, a practical, division of attention. Both are absolutely necessary.

(March 10, 1923)

There are so many side lights on an important report that cannot always be put in a report, aren't there? That report of the Public Welfare committee of the Federation of Women's Clubs. It spoke efficient and wise words about Chattahoochee. But it could not say very well one of the things which the committee members brought back as part of their own memories. The most poignant thing to them was the women's ward, where women of all degrees of mental unbalance are kept. It is kept clean, of course, and the women's clothes are clean. But their uniforms, the poor pitiful uniforms of

women who once loved beautiful things, are so patched and torn and un-becoming. That is a thing which women, rather than men, would notice, isn't it? They could guess what it might mean to some of the women not to have a little personal niceness.

Yet the inherent courage that lies, like hope, at the very bottom of the treasure box of humankind they found prevailing. In one corner of the long ward, the bare, institutional ward of such places, one little quiet woman sits, always starting new crochet patterns of delicate intricacy, which she never quite remembers to finish. She crochets diligently. Never lifting her eyes to the figure or two which sometimes clamor up and down between the beds, hair wild, arms tossing. "We get rough here, sometimes," she explained mildly to one of the visiting women. "It is hard to help get-ting rough. But there—I'm not going to think about that. I'm going to think everything is pretty. I'm going to make things real pretty. I like to make pretty things, don't you?" And her mild blue eyes slipped unseeingly over the other women and went back to her delicate crochet pattern. Yet how could the committee put that sort of bravery into a mere report?

(March 30, 1923)

There's many a man who likes a laugh about women who's never been able to act differently from the way one of them brought him up.

The more you read books about women written by men, the less sur-prised you are that men don't believe that women are people.

(June 15, 1923)

∽ 5 ∽ Social Progressive

In all her forms of written work—newspaper, short stories, and books—it was The Galley in which Douglas was most prolifically vocal about social injustice in the world. She wanted to alert her readers to humanity's shortcomings and awaken in them a sense of social responsibility.

Throughout her adult life, Douglas dedicated herself to human causes. It was, in fact, her humanitarian spirit that turned her interest toward environmental protection. She was remarkably forceful when she decried the maldistribution of wealth between the rich and the poor, which she blamed on the greed of men. She had first been introduced to poverty by her Wellesley economics professor, Emily Greene Balch, a future Nobel Peace Prize winner who liked to tromp her students through the streets of Boston's most neglected neighborhoods.[1] Douglas's exposure to Balch's work on Boston made her sensitive to the deplorable social realities born from Miami's rapid growth. Her bosses at the *Herald* discouraged writing about squalor, and others contended that poverty was a natural part of any city's existence. Douglas abhorred such "willful blindness." High on her columnist's agenda was cajoling the city to take action toward improving public health and child welfare. In 1922, she took the initiative in this area when she organized a milk fund, with the sponsorship of the *Herald,* for babies of poor families. The milk fund benefited only white children, however.

While the exclusion of blacks was not necessarily the decision of Douglas, her views on race were traditional. She opposed the Ku Klux Klan and violence against blacks in an era when racial violence was rife, but she assented to the second-class position to which white-dominated society had assigned its black citizens. Looking to the state level, Douglas denounced convict leasing, the practice by state and local authorities of hiring out con-

Convicted on a trumped-up charge of vagrancy, 22-year-old Martin Tabert was
sentenced to serve time at a prisoner-lease camp, where he was beaten to death in
1921. Outraged, Douglas composed a poem about the incident to alert the public
to the inhumanity of the convict-lease system, which the Florida legislature voted
to abolish in 1923. Courtesy of Florida State Archives.

vict labor, often black, to private concerns. Convict leasing in the South
was notorious for countenancing slavelike labor, brutality, neglect, and
death. Douglas's proudest moment as a columnist resulted from her au-
thorship of "Martin Tabert of North Dakota." Reprinted at the request of
Herald readers, the poem related the story of a young white man beaten to
death in a labor camp. It was subsequently read before the Florida legisla-
ture, where lawmakers were impelled to debate the future of the convict-
leasing system. Ultimately, they outlawed both corporal punishment and
leasing.[2]

As a journalist committed to free expression, Douglas was equally out-
spoken against censorship. She showed no patience for Anthony Com-
stock, head of the New York Society for the Suppression of Vice, and U.S.

Attorney General A. Mitchell Palmer, whose attempts to impose upon society moral standards to his liking endangered the constitutional rights of citizens. Professional self-interest underlay her commitment to the First Amendment, but she also understood that the least free to speak in society were the dispossessed. Thirty-two years after leaving the newspaper business, she became a charter member of the first American Civil Liberties Union chapter organized below the Mason-Dixon line.[3]

Because Douglas was always quick to exercise her constitutional rights, her critical voice is earnest and strong in the following passages. They address a wide range of social concerns, from public health to race relations.

> With Thanks to the Purple Cow.
> I never saw a Bolshevist
> I never hope to see one
> But this I'll tell you anyhow
> That what with deportation and jail sentences and the
> condition of Russia and unpopularity and one hundred
> percent Americanism and the attitude of the Saturday
> Evening Post, I'd a whole lot rather see than be one.
> *(March 7, 1920)*

In place of hounding out the authors of books whose subject matter they are not sure is immoral until the policeman on the corner or the waitress tell them so, we might suggest to the earnest consideration of the Society for the Suppression of Vice the price list of some of our best restaurants.
(April 13, 1920)

The greatest harm that the rampant reformer does is to insist that wickedness is of such tremendous importance.

Too much money is one of the annoyances to which too few people have been subjected.
(April 24, 1920)

Book Notes In Brief.

It is with the utmost pleasure that we report that the Society for the Suppression of Vice, which has committed more crimes against literature in America than were ever committed against liberty, has been forced to pay $2,500 to a book agent who was arrested by them for selling Gautier's "Mademoiselle de Maupin," in an English translation. The jury refused to find the book vicious.

(May 18, 1920)

("The present high prices may be directly attributed to the desire of the people to spend money lavishly."—Statement by a large manufacturer in a recent news item.)

> When a profiteer's engaged in his employment
> A-raising the price of meat and coal,
> Don't imagine that he really finds enjoyment;
> Making money's really hurtful to his soul.
> His anguish he with difficulty smothers
> When tenants all insist he raise their rent.
> Oh, a profiteer has feelings same as others;
> He'd be happy if he never made a cent.
>
> When a profiteer is raking in his profits
> His sobs and tears are pitiful to view;
> He'd love to sell his stock by knocking off it
> His costs, plus all expenses, taxes, too.
> But the public still insists upon his taking
> The money that their industry has won.
> Oh, taking every little dollar with another,
> The profiteer is not a happy man.

(June 24, 1920)

A Simple Solution.
The trouble with the U.S.A.
 It's very plain to me,
Is wanting more than it should need,
 All very unlike me.

My wants are modest, plain and few,
 Of fine simplicity.
I'd like to have a house in town
 With bedrooms only ten,
A modest country place, as well,
 With golf links and a hen,
With simple milk from simple cows
 And fat pigs in a pen.

The car I'd choose would not be loud
 Or overly ornate;
A limousine in blue and then
 A quiet Rolls Royce Eight,
A runabout for shopping trips
 Or catching trains when late.

For yachts I think just one would do,
 Some sober thing in black,
About three hundred tons or so
 That leaves a foamy track,
For little trips to Bimini
 Or else to Spain and back.

And with some dresses, just a score;
 Five velvet bathing suits,
Some riding clothes, three evening coats
 And purple pumps and shoes and boots;
I think I'd be quite satisfied
 And ask no substitution.

In men, also, my tastes are mild
 And suited to my means,
I'd have a few for dances and,
 For contrast, one in jeans.
Three cultured ones for theaters
 And five for moonlight scenes.

And so I think that if, like me,
 This country wanted less
And made itself be satisfied
 With simple ways and dress,

We'd hear no more of strikes and things
 Or national restlessness.

(July 16, 1920)

But at the same time, about all the recreation nowadays you get without transgressing some law or other or getting the Moral Guardians down on you is leaving the windows open and letting it rain in.

(August 11, 1920)

Apropos of the Society for the Suppression of Vice and Mr. [U.S. Attorney General] A. Mitchell Palmer and several other institutions we could mention here but won't, it is interesting to remember that Thoreau said that good books were those which made us dangerous to existing institutions.

(August 14, 1920)

We have long been accustomed in this country to the struggle between capital and labor, and we are used to the vituperative methods of either toward the other. And yet a study of what is influencing both brings us to the conclusion that each has the same motives, one neither better nor worse than the other. Capital wants to keep what it has. Labor wants to get what capital has. Why one should be an altruistic aim and the other a selfish one, is more than we can see. Capital dresses up its desires to retain what it has in various high-sounding phrases, "normalcy," "prosperity," "intelligent guidance," and labor does the same by claiming brotherhood, and the superiority of the masses over the classes. And yet in America today the difference between capital and labor is so slight that it is positively interchangeable, the laborer often becoming a capitalist and the capitalist often becoming a laborer.

(September 2, 1920)

If this world should get perfectly good it's a horrible thing to think how many reformers and uplifters would have to take to running elevators.

(September 12, 1920)

There are more reformers in the world than ever before for the simple reason that the older the world grows the more people there are who discover how much easier it is to reform others than it is to reform themselves.

(October 3, 1920)

America stands first today among the number of purely humorous nations. It can be taken in no other way, when you consider the wild contrast between what it thinks and what it does, what it feels and how it acts. If you prefer to hold its great national inconsistencies as tragedy, that's your affair. It is tragedy for many. But surely the spirit of pure comedy has assailed whatever it is that shapes our career. Our constitution is founded on the idea of liberty, we sing about it, we orate about it, we put it on our currency. And yet in America public opinion has so taken away the freedom from speech that the postmaster general suppresses novels, the courts suppress opinions and the average public, by being impatient of everything but the concrete, like baseball, the HCL [high cost of living] and the new styles, suppress everything but the most banal and humdrum of ideas.

Debs is still in jail for speaking but Hard-Boiled Smith, the worst hated man in the A.E.F. [American Expeditionary Force] is released from prison before his term is up.[4]

We send thousands of dollars worth of supplies to Armenian victims of Turkish atrocities while we lynch and burn negroes in America without fair trial.

We believe in democracy because we think that all men are equal and it results in insisting that all men shall be alike.

We think that no country in the world is so enlightened as ours, with so much education and progress. But great American artists are few and far between and those we recognize gained their greatest reputations in Europe before we would admit it.

We believe that the voice of the people is the voice of God and yet it is the common understanding that only money talks.

The greatest office in the service of the government, the presidency, is gained by the system of dividing all citizens into two classes, Republicans and Democrats, although no one knows why, campaigning for months to select candidates, neither of whom are the real choice of various conventions, and, by listening to long and fulsome orations by each on the great-

ness of America, the value of democracy, the advantages of a free country, trying to decide which will be better fitted to see that the laws are carried out, to command the army and navy, to make treaties with foreign countries and pass on the state of Congress. That nothing is determined by this method except that one candidate has a louder voice than another, or can string together more phrases which sound extremely well on a platform, or can raise more money among his adherents than the other, we do not seem to recognize. The people can do no wrong.

We believe that we have the keenest sense of humor of any nation on earth. But we have never yet laughed at ourselves.

(October 7, 1920)

It has been suggested that the reason that Henry Ford[5] is getting so vicious about the Jews is that nowadays they are buying only real automobiles.

(December 23, 1920)

Mrs. Carrie Chapman Catt[6] says that she does not recall one time in history when a great reform was brought about by a political party. Mrs. Catt would approach more nearly to exactitude if she would confine her remarks to the statement that she does not recall one time in history when a great reform was brought about.

(March 12, 1921)

The people who have quantities of leisure generally have taken it from others who have none.

(March 19, 1921)

The teachers of West Virginia are not allowed to attend dances. The teachers of New York are not allowed to hold political opinions different from those of the local party in power. Teachers out west are not allowed to teach any fact in history which may seem to the school board of prosperous farmers not to be 100 per cent American. Taking one consideration with another, it is a marvel to us that there are any teachers left to be underpaid.

(April 7, 1921)

The more we see the various and excited preparations that are made against Red outrages that never come off on May first, the more we think May Day should come on the first of April.

(May 5, 1921)

Perhaps after all, the real reason for the enthusiasm to be a reformer is that it is a quick way of appearing to be a saint by emphasizing the sins of others.

(April 20, 1922)

From a Journalist's Day Book.

Wednesday, September 27.

There ought to be some sort of part-time school here for the training of colored girls to be competent domestic servants. Where we get the idea that running a house and doing the cooking is a job that does not require intelligence I don't understand. Yet it is a highly specialized profession for which our system of education offers no preparation. We ought to have some institution here where intelligent and willing colored girls, who already work in homes, could be sent for a few afternoons a week for practical training in direct connection with their work in the private home. I know of one right now who would be tremendously benefited by it. And in that connection there is that excellent plan of the Antioch school, in which two students work together, one in school and one on the job, for something like six weeks. After that they alternate and the other one goes to school and the other on the job, so that neither the work of school or business, whatever it is, is interrupted. The boys' work is made directly related, both to study and to life, and by working the thing in pairs the two maintain a constant eager interest in both. Why that couldn't be worked here for training in domestic work I don't see. And, goodness knows, it would be tremendously worth while to the householder to maintain it.

They say there isn't anything new under the sun, but in Georgia they have convicted some white men for lynching a negro. The New South is overtaking the Old South so fast that you can hear it whizz.

(October 1, 1922)

Ellsworth Huntington of Yale has produced a chart of the stars for the next 70,000 years, or thereabouts. It is described in a circular which says one should get the chart "If you want to know what is going to happen during the next 70,000 years." We personally don't need the chart. We know exactly what is going to happen in the next 70,000 years. When any especially good idea for the aid and assistance of the human race is timidly put forward by its originator, it will immediately be suppressed by all the leading citizens on the grounds that it is "idealistic."

(October 7, 1922)

What we can't understand is, how the people who decide what is or is not immoral in a book ever escape the awful consequences of reading them.

(October 11, 1922)

The great problem of whether the newspaper should print only the news that is considered fit to print, or whether it should print everything that the public seems to enjoy, like murders and suicides and riots and cheery little evidences of our very common human nature, still wages on. Every once and so often some one comes out with a statement about the corruption of the public by the yellow press, and the churches, especially, get excited about it. The idea seems to be that the newspapers, by printing the story of a crime, incite other people to go and do likewise. They forget a little that human nature is older than the newspapers and that the proper study of mankind is man.

(November 12, 1922)

A free discussion of ideas seems to be about the hardest thing there is to get in this country. The minute you say something someone else does not agree with, his cry is that you ought not to be allowed to talk at all. I like best the old motto of Voltaire—at least I think it was Voltaire—who said, "I disagree with every word you say, but I will defend to the death your right to say it." It seems to me that is the only possible atmosphere in which men can learn to use what gray matter they have been given.

(November 21, 1922)

Cities and Children.

Cities are the poetry which America makes.

The old world made cathedrals for its poetry.

We build cities.

But they are not cathedral cities.

We come together in them with no one-ness of spirit.

Our altars are smoke-stained,

Our columns are steel and brick,

Our choir is a thousand clanging hammers,

The rattle of the cement mixer,

The shriek of noon whistles.

But still cities are the poetry which America shall make.

White cities in sunshine are lifting in Florida.

In New York, Illinois, California,

The mastodon cities lift in mist and clangor their dullness.

Through their streets the life of their people streams turgid.

Think of the smoky grimness of factory cities,

Think of the reek and stain of stockyard cities,

The salt wind and the hooting of ships and the clattering of
 steam hoists

Of the cities that front oceans with dinginess,

Green seas with squalor.

Yet the poetry of America shall be cities,

Cities, new cities, shining and splendid,

Cities, and then the children in cities.

When the thoughts of the people shall turn to their cities,

When the people's thought shall turn,

Then will the cities answer.

How can they build clean when their thoughts are dingy?

How can they build beauty from iron minds?

The color of our streets stains forever the lives of the children

And mutilated lives of the children flow upward

Into uglier cities, into more harsh cities,

Into dirt and refuse and brickyards and tenement streets.

Cities are the poetry that America makes.

Ugly poetry, harsh poetry, bad poetry.

When shall the thoughts of the people turn to their cities?

Only a little while and the harshness could be strength.
Only a little while, and the ugliness could be clean and
 forceful.
Only a little thinking, a little thinking together,
All together, all of us, working and thinking together,
And the new children could go singing through new streets.
Children and cities, cities and children, these shall be the
 poetry which America makes.

(December 24, 1922)

The "Journal of Social Forces," published by the University of North Caro-
lina Press at Chapel Hill, N.C., is in every way a splendid organ of modern
social thought. It is a publication of which the whole South can be proud
because it is so thoroughly dedicated to the idea that the best that is known
and thought in the world must be more widely known, must be more easily
diffused among all of us who are building a tomorrow for our region and
our community. Among the subjects discussed in the January *Journal* are
"Teaching and Research in the Social Sciences," "Public Welfare and Social
Work," "Conferences for Social Work," "The Church and Social Service,"
"Inter-Racial Co-operation," "County and Country Life Programs," and
"The Work of Women's Organizations." "Effective Democracy" is a very
splendid editorial by Dr. Howard Odum.

(December 30, 1922)

It is interesting to note, in those published telephone interviews, and those
about "My Ideal City" how much good will and high purpose people have
for the benefit of their city in general, but how vague, on the whole, they
are. In all this discussion of improvements, for instance, only once has one
very fundamental thing been suggested, an idea which is a very modern
one and which is by far the most up-to-date method of handling all prob-
lems relating to dependent, defective and delinquent children yet devised.
That is a county organization for child welfare, which was mentioned as far
as I can remember, only once. Yet every body ought to know about that.
We need it badly in Dade County this very minute.

(January 30, 1923)

One of the latest ideas which seems to be sweeping Congress and some legislatures is that of erecting monuments to negro mammies. This sentiment is, of course, delightful, but somehow we can't help feeling that a more widespread interest in vocational and industrial schools for the descendants of the negro mammies would be a lot more to the point. It is curious how far sentimentality will take people where common sense cannot make them budge one step.

(February 9, 1923)

We are coming to see that if an engineer, by sitting down with a pencil and paper, can create a great and lovely machine which will actually produce miracles, that other engineers, social engineers, if you like, can sit down with pencil and paper and plan a better life than the one we live today, can plan a system which will be lovelier and freer for all men, in which they can be safe from mutilations, of the mind as of the body, free to live finely and beautifully, with room to grow rightly as plants grow in a well-prepared garden.

There is no rhapsody in this. Already we are beginning to see, a little dimly, that this can be so. We are beginning to see, vaguely, that a city can be planned and built according to plan, in which such practical things as sewerage and light and water and traffic and parks and play ground can be the best possible for the well-being of the public. We are beginning to see that we can not only plan and build and live in beautiful and efficient cities, towns, villages, rural districts, but that we can make whole generations of people yet unborn who will be free of disease, free of mutilations of body, free of mental illness, free of those tendencies to crime and disorder which stunted lives, stunted and diseased minds always bring with them. Vaguely, we are realizing that we are not only building cities but we are building the people who will live in the cities, the people who are to come after us, unwilling inheritors of what we are to give them as a way of life and as a means of living.

These things are, and of eternal justice must be, the public concern. And not the concern of that small body of elected persons whom we, by scribbling upon pieces of paper, put into official places for short periods of time, but the concern of the true public, which is all of us. The time must come,

and is coming, when the minds of people must be turned to these consid-
erations as problems more intimate to them and their children than the
problems of social prestige, of games, of dress, of sport or even of money
making. Our thinking must change itself over into a new feeling about
people, about our own people and the people whose lives a thousand years
hence we are creating today. We are going to be made to realize, in the next
hundred years, that the way a child has of making the world his life, and of
making his life rich and fine thereby, must be made safe for the adult, must
be the way people will have of living.

(February 11, 1923)

Wayside Children and Cities.

The children in the little towns
 Of grey slabbed shacks in piney places
Have puzzled eyes of blue or brown
 And wondering looks on freckled faces
To see the shining cars roar by
To shining cities beyond sky.

It seems so strange to them to think
 That other children, far away,
Live in great houses, white or pink,
 And walk on pavement every day.
Some day, they whisper, they will go
And see the marvels cities show.

And then they'll roar and honk and hoot
 By other shabby houses
And make the hens and children scoot
 And laugh as fright their speed arouses.
It is so fine and big and grand
To roar like that through all the land.

And yet I wonder if the white
 And shining cities that they dream,
Will be to them so fine and bright
 When they can hear the city's scream?

I wonder if the city's whine
Will seem more sweet than wind in pine?
Yet how should wayside children guess
 That wayside shacks in piney places
Share with the city's wilderness
 Its ugliness, its stupid faces?
How should they know what new dreams rise
Like finer cities, near skies?

That dream that poet-builders dare
 Who see as one the whole of green vast
Of cities, wilds, and thoroughfare
 in equal beauty, planned at last
To pledge all children, starved and dull
life more abundant, beautiful.

Nothing could be more encouraging than the growing interest in Miami
and Dade County in matters relating to public health of children. You can
have the most beautiful city in the world as appearance goes, the streets
may be clean and shining, the avenues broad and tree lined, the public
buildings dignified, adequate and well kept, and all the physical facilities
for the richer life of the people, like schools and concert halls and libraries
and churches, but if you have a weak or inadequate health department, or
a public opinion lax on the subject, all the splendors of your city will have
no value. The condition of the public health is the indication of the degree
of civilization in that city. You can spend thousands and thousands of dol-
lars yearly on education, on securing the best possible teachers and the
most advanced methods of study, but if the children who go to school un-
der compulsory laws are filled with hookworm or malaria or tuberculosis or
influenza, your money had much better be thrown in the bay. A sick child
cannot learn anything. An undernourished child cannot learn anything.
And a child hampered in its studies by the lack of proper sanitation or
health of its home, cannot learn anything. The only way to insure a sound
body politic is to insure sound bodies for citizens. And that is the idea that
has at last caught and held in the public imagination in Miami. That is why
the doctors and the dentists who have pledged their support to a child

health center are receiving the co-operation of the women and of all public-spirited citizens to see that it is made actual.

But it is a little startling to learn that Miami leads almost all the rest of Florida in this. Mrs. Laura Jean Reid, who has been making a survey of Florida health conditions, says that this aroused public opinion in Miami is the most definite hope for improved conditions which she has found in all Florida. That looks bad for Florida. It looks bad for Miami, because Miami needs a lot more than just the beginning interest. It only convinces us that this matter of public health, and especially child health, must become more important to all of us or our hopes for city planning, our hopes for a greater city are doomed.

(February 23, 1923)

No king could, even in Egyptian days, command the tremendous forces which answer a push of the button for us. We are growing accustomed to this feeling of greater power. We send our voices nonchalantly across continents. We motor to New York in ten days. We go to Europe in a week. We command power of checking disease and of destroying nations, of living under water and in the air, which would have crisped the greatest Roman emperor with envy. And as we study the increasing ratio of such discoveries of new uses of power it looks as if the next two or three generations were to see an increase in that proportion which will far outstrip anything that we can know today. There is no reason at all to doubt it. Man is about to become more powerful than his wildest dreams of power. The magnitude of the force at his command is positively bewildering. Yet to grasp and handle the new forces which will be set to his hand, the very mind of man must increase its tempo. The new art, the new literature, which so bewilders people of the old school, has been touched by this increased mental tempo. It is keeping up minds to the recognitions which are awaiting it. The problem of these immense new forces which man will control, or rather, man's problem, will be how to use these forces wisely for the betterment, and not the destruction, of himself and of mankind. It will take a new kind of thinking, as well as a new speed of thought. We will have to have a new type of social mind, a popular opinion, which will begin to see clearly that there can be no good upon earth which does not include the good of every

human being on the earth. With such powers as even now, man is begin-
ning to feel the old miseries of mankind have little excuse for being. Pov-
erty and disease are not more powerful than the new forces which man can
control. Wrong and suffering wait only the turning of the new power upon
them to be changed. What we need is the fundamental realization that so-
cial justice must be the only utilizer of such forces as are already dimly out-
lined, and that expansion of life for the individual must, somehow, follow
from this energy which awaits man in every sunbeam, in every drop of
water, in every atom. That the human race, mazed and bewildered by the
scope of the powers which it is learning how to set free, will not destroy
itself like a child with a buzz saw, can only be prevented by the strengthen-
ing in this generation, of this ultimate social attitude of mind. Man will be
forced at last to live together in some sort of harmony, in some sort of tol-
erance and understanding because he must, or perish. It is an inevitable
conclusion, if one faces this thing calmly.

(March 2, 1923)

The most public-spirited newspaper in Florida which we have found this
week is that valiant weekly called the *Kissimmee Valley Gazette.* On its front
page it carried an excellent story of the opening of the first curb market in
that town, and on its editorial page it carried two columns of plain lan-
guage in which it called upon the Ku Klux Klan, and the anti-Ku Klux
Klan of that place to forget it and the name, turn themselves back into
ordinary good citizens, and get together for the good of the whole region.
This is good talk and plain talk and courageous talk, but the best of it is it
is rooted and grounded on the only possible common sense. Probably nei-
ther the Klansmen nor the Anti-Klansmen of Kissimmee will like it very
well.

(March 3, 1923)

It has seemed to be the general idea that nothing could be done about stu-
pid people. The world, apparently, simply has to be made up of a large
number of stupid ones and a smaller number of intelligent ones, and the
intelligent ones are completely helpless to do anything about it. All they
can do, according to this way of thinking, is to protect themselves by the

brains as much as possible and let the stupid keep on being stupid and the world keep on being generally muddled. But you know it is a very comforting thing to realize that there is another way of thinking about it than that. Apparently we are discovering for the first time that there are all sorts of reasons why people are stupid, or criminal or backward. And very many of these reasons can be prevented or changed, if the rest of the people are intelligent enough. That is what the new ideas about eugenics are, as was so well brought out at the Woman's club the other day.[7] Eugenics is merely the key to the next generation. It has to do with those agencies which will improve or impair the inborn health and quality of children yet unborn. It means that as soon as any generation realizes its tremendous power sufficiently it can produce a succeeding generation which will be very much higher in the grade of health, intelligence and potential social value. People cannot be changed very often by anything after they have lived years and years. But people can very often be changed before they are born, or before their fathers and mothers are born. That is why the subject of the new eugenics is a very important one for Miami people to consider, as Miami people are considering. We are not only building a town which we hope will be a success as a city in a few years, and be rich and progressive. But we hope that we will build a city which will produce finer and finer generations of citizens, a city fit for the best possible children to be brought up in, which will help them to be more intelligent, more healthful, more sound and free of bad inheritances, than any other city we know.

(March 28, 1923)

Everybody says he or she had no idea that leasing convicts was still practiced in Florida. But great snakes, it's your state isn't it? Who else knows if you don't? And how many other things like that are going on that you don't know about? Did you know that because of no industrial school for boys in this county, boys have to be kept, very often, by the private charity of the probation officer, because there is no other place for them besides jail or the girl's school, which is overcrowded? Did you know that at Chattahoochee, the state insane asylum, while they have excellent physical and surgical care for mental disorders, they have absolutely no psychiatric ward, as the best ones all do now, for the proper treatment of mental disorders which have

not an organic cause? Did you know that there is a religious orphanage for children in North Florida which leases the children out for work? Did you know that the children of the rural districts of Florida, over 75 percent, have hook worms?[8] No, this is not all related to the death of a convict, and yet it is, too. Because these institutions are all state institutions, and hence the affair of the citizens of the state, whose lack of knowledge about them is the reason for their continuance. If that state board of public welfare goes through at Tallahassee, then we will have the proper means for knowing about these things, and seeing that the name of Florida gets clear of notoriety which it has undoubtedly deserved.

(April 18, 1923)

The [Martin] Tabert case is doing a good deal for Florida. It makes us realize that just because a state has institutions of one kind or another, penal or philanthropic, is not enough. The people of the state, the sovereign state itself, must become the guardian of every one of the inmates in all institutions, or else, with the excuse of public apathy, other such acts of social injustice can easily occur. There are, for instance, in Marianna, the industrial school for delinquent boys, exactly sixty boys who had to be committed there, not because they are delinquents, but because they are dependent, because there is no other place for the juvenile courts to send them. These sixty future citizens of the sovereign state of Florida are therefore thrust, by the state itself, into direct contact with boys who are actually delinquent, who have criminal tendencies, some of them. And the state later will have to reap the reward of that. Yet nobody knows about that, because there is no Board of Public Welfare to make such things public.

A very tragic phase, for Florida, of the death of youth Tabert, was revealed by the aged senator from North Dakota who helped start the agitation in the state. It seems he has for years been a regular and devoted winter visitor to Florida and he has known, equally for years, the Tabert family. It was because of his constant praise of Florida that young Tabert decided to come here, on his trip around the country. In North Dakota they do not send boys to prison camps or penitentiaries for catching rides on trains. So that the North Dakota man who is now in Tallahassee taking a large part in the revelations there is worn with grief, feeling that he was largely respon-

sible. But it goes farther than that. The responsibility for conditions in prison camps rests on every citizen of Florida, and, to a large measure, our regular winter residents of this state, who forget that, because we are the world's finest playground, we are still a state where men and women live and work, and where acts of horrible social injustice may go on all the longer just because of the indifference of residents and visitors alike. There are institutions, behind the charming atmosphere of the playground, which the playground cannot longer overlook.

(April 19, 1923)

Martin Tabert of North Dakota.
(Ballad to be sung in a minor key,
but at the end with shouts.)

Martin Tabert of North Dakota is walking Florida now.
O children, hark to his footsteps coming, for he's walking soft
 and slow.
Through the piney woods and the cypress hollows,
A wind creeps up and it's him it follows.
Martin Tabert of North Dakota, walking Florida now.

They took him out to the convict camp, and he's walking
 Florida now.
O children, the tall pines stood and heard him when he was
 moaning low.
The other convicts, they stood around him,
When the length of the black strap cracked and found him.
Martin Tabert of North Dakota. And he's walking Florida now.

They nailed his coffin boards together and he's walking Florida
 now.
O children, the dark night saw where they buried him, buried
 him, buried him low.
And the tall pines heard where they went to hide him,
And the wind crept up to moan beside him,
Martin Tabert of North Dakota. And he's walking Florida now.

The whip is still in the convict camps, for Florida's stirring
 now.

Children, from Key West to Pensacola you can hear the great
wind go.
The wind that he roused when he lay dying,
The angry voice of Florida crying,
 "Martin Tabert of North Dakota,
 Martin Tabert of North Dakota,
 Martin Tabert of North Dakota.
 You can rest from your walking now!"

(April 20, 1923; reprinted April 25, 1923)

The remedy for this wretched state of affairs is not only the killing of the
peonage system, but the establishment by the state of a department of pub-
lic welfare which shall be responsible for everything which goes on in state
institutions of all kinds. The peonage system has been called to our atten-
tion because of the death of a man. Why wait until death before we find
out what is going on wherever the state maintains its necessary affairs? As it
is now there is absolutely no way of checking up or finding out. Even the
governor must call special investigations to find out things which he should
know at all times. The newspapers of the state should be able to find out
conditions at all times. Only a department of public welfare, which practi-
cally all the other states have, can do this work.

These are important days for Florida at the legislature. It seems incred-
ible that private agencies should oppose not only the peonage bill but the
creation of a public welfare board, for the purpose of letting the public find
out what is going on in its own institutions, and assisting in good work
wherever it is going on, as well as bringing about a better and closer relation
between the public and the people in its institutions. A fight is apparently
being made, but it is one of those losing affairs. If the forces of reaction win
this time, they will not win next time. The women are determined that
never again shall the name of the state be blotted as it is now, through the
public ignorance and indifference. That the finest minds of its leading men
statesmen are fighting with women, makes it doubly sure. These are the
great days for the new Florida.

(April 25, 1923)

A Few Good Hates.

I'd hate to be the senators
 Who own the convict camps,
I'd hate to think I had men flogged
 To buy me postage stamps,
I'd hate a peon predilection
 I know I'd lose the next election.

I'd hate to be the public man
 Who thinks that flogging's fine
And pleads so in the house
 For black straps soaked in brine.
I'd doubt if my career'd recover.

I'd hate to be the editor
 Who wrote the flippant pieces,
About the awful criminal
 And lovely convict leases.
I'd hate to have that sort of head.
 I think my paper'd not get read.

I'd hate to be the citizen
 Who thinks injustice funny
And wishes we would stop this talk
 Because of tourists' money.
I think the season would be dearer
 If Florida were New Siberia.

It is awful for a columnist to try to be humorous these days, with men standing in the house of the legislature of the state of Florida and upholding the thing which has brought shame to this state all over the length and breadth of the country. The only possible answer to the protest of the sovereign state of North Dakota to the sovereign state of Florida, on that subject, was such a rising on the name of every public official, unanimously, as those legislative halls has never seen before. They should have risen as one man, as the representatives of one aroused and shamed state and said, in tones that should have rung all over the north and the south and the west,

tones which would have carried to every newspaper headline in the country the one possible answer, "North Dakota, this terrible injustice for which we stand responsible and any other thing of its kind, so help us God, shall never happen again." That is the only answer, that is the only possible answer, which would have changed the attitude of the rest of the states to the state of Florida. It would have shown the world that the people of Florida would not for one moment tolerate the opprobrium that was once cast on Belgium for the Congo, Russia for Siberia or Germany for Louvain. And today men are standing in Tallahassee quibbling about whether or not the lash hurts. These are difficult days in which to try to be humorous.

(May 1, 1923)

We are all conscious of the new urge to make something better of society than as it was handed to us. We are going through a period when all sorts of quack remedies for social betterment are being forced upon us, all sorts of isms and ologies, social theories, industrial theories. Yet we cannot determine their value until we study man himself in light of actual knowledge.

What we are really beginning to see is that democracy is the only possible method, but that we have not yet learned how to bring it about. We are holding back all sorts of fine things, all sorts of improvements, not because we do not understand or approve of them in theory, but because we simply have not yet learned to live together in fact. Labor and capital, all our political problems, our social problems, the question of proper education and proper government, are hindered because we have not yet set ourselves to know how to live with our fellow men.

(May 10, 1923)

The Children of a Town.

What are the children of a town
But hostages for its renown?

What are the pavements where they play
But patterns for its future day?
What are the crowded rooms they know
But dreary paths where towns must go?

What are the sallow cheeks and pale
But signs to mark where cities fall?

What is the soiled youth in their eyes,
But blots upon the city's skies?

Oh robbed, hurt children everywhere,
You are the future we must share.

You cannot do any investigative work in this town, whether it is for under-fed children or what, without realizing that Miami needs a lot of things which hinge very much on the idea of a city plan. The appalling thing to me was the number of little dinky shacks, where people pay as high as five dollars a week for almost no conveniences at all, and which are tucked be-hind other houses, or other shacks. We take so much for granted the idea that Miami is so young and clean and splendid, with all its natural beauty, that we could not possibly have the overcrowding and the congestion of older northern cities. And yet the fifty-foot front lot and the desire for rent-als is rapidly making potential slums in several places in our city. The shack of today is the slum of tomorrow and we can't be too quick to realize it. You find sick people living in shacks like that, too, tubercular especially.

And we have absolutely no provision in this city for the proper isolation of tubercular cases.[9] What do you think about that?

(June 16, 1923)

The most stimulating and revealing thing you can do, if you want some-thing stimulating in summer here, is to look over the records of the city health department and discover how much even a new city like Miami needs in the way of better care for babies and nursing for children. The question of social welfare work for a young city like this is very much like the question of the care of baby teeth. The old theory was that it didn't matter whether the first teeth were decayed or broken, because the second set was coming right in any way. Now we know that young cities are like the first set of teeth. If they are started right, the second set will have a fair chance to be good. But if they are allowed to be bad, so will the second.

Miami is just about ready to cut her second set of teeth but a lot will depend on the condition of the first ones.

(June 17, 1923)

> The Versemaker's Problem.
> The sky is blue, the sun is bright,
> The air is sweet and soft as silk
> But what new poetry can one write,
> When hungry babies cry for milk?

A discussion arose in this office recently as to the looks of an underfed child, and it came over me with a shock that there are very many people, and especially very many business men, who have probably never noticed underfed children, or come in contact with them, enough to know what effect underfeeding has upon the appearance, especially the facial appearance. Perhaps I can enlighten them a little. I have seen tiny babies in the last stages of starvation, brought in perhaps to some American Red Cross station in the Balkans who were probably the most hideous things it is possible to look on. Because starvation does to a normally fat baby face just what old age does to a man. When the fat is gone the face is all withered and the bony structures of the temples and the cheeks stand out sharply, unnaturally in what should be a smooth baby face. Then the skin is often not so much white as that unpleasant, unhealthy yellow of old parchment, the skull is prominent and the whole look is a tiny, miserable ancient man. Then, again, you must know that a starving baby, a really starving baby does not cry. It is perfectly silent, because it has not enough strength to cry. The feeble flame of its life is very low, almost flickering. But I have seen babies brought in like that, with the added complication of a terrible skin disease such as, thank fortune, you do not often find here, changed in a few weeks into splendid, normal, rosy, fat, chuckling babies, hollering their heads off at the first twinge of hunger, just because they were fed milk. No medicine, no doctoring, just milk, a little at a time dropped into those withered bare gums. I have not yet seen any baby in the last stages of starvation in Miami, thank goodness. But I have seen babies and children, who

are obviously underfed, so underfed that you would think that anyone who saw them could see the need immediately. Anaemic children are generally undernourished, the doctors say, unless, of course, there is some sort of physical complication. But when in the last school health inspection held in this city it was found that there were over eighty cases of pernicious anaemia in three schools alone, then surely we should begin to realize that there is a situation here which must be met. The Parent-Teacher Association has realized this long ago and they have struggled to have milk sold in the schools. The doctors and the nurses of the city realize it, and the social workers. So that if the children of well-to-do people are shown to be suffering from undernourishment, how much more likely is it that the children of poor people are? And it is not just a question of likelihood. It is a question of actual fact, because the cases exist and are known.

(June 21, 1923)

All members of the Rotary Club who subscribed a dollar to the Herald Milk Fund are respectfully informed that if they want to send us four more dollars to put with it we will credit them with five dollars and put their names in the paper separately besides, just showing to what great lengths we are willing to go to get these fifty-three and more children of South Florida fed.

(June 23, 1923)

⤳ 6 ⤳ *Intellectual*

Marjory Stoneman Douglas was able to comment on a broad range of issues because she read widely and because she reflected upon and absorbed much of what she read. When in 1926 she built her house, which she called her workshop, she stocked it with two things: used furniture and books. She was known for being able to direct visitors to a passage on the topic of discussion from any one of those books. Friends and colleagues remember that even in her nineties, she betrayed an intimidating intellect and a steel-trap memory.[1] She never intentionally tried to intimidate others, but she never suffered fools gladly, as she was wont to say. She believed that before one discussed an issue, one should be educated on that issue.

Douglas educated herself primarily with books. She acquired a love for reading and a quest for knowledge at an early age and sharpened her intellectual skills at Wellesley. Throughout her adult life, she occupied herself with poetry, fiction, history, the classics, science, politics, and anthropology. She even read *Social Forces*, the premier sociology journal published at the University of North Carolina at Chapel Hill by the famous sociologist Howard Odum.

She possessed a nimble and penetrating mind, as her father soon learned after their reunion, that allowed her to discuss a multitude of subjects and ideas. So committed was Douglas to intellectual pursuits that, after her marriage to Kenneth, she concluded that for herself an intimate relationship with a man was not a possibility. Love and sex, she noted in her autobiography, were needless distractions from cognitive stimulation and imaginative thought. Consistent with such beliefs, she kept diaries not of her daily experiences but of her musings. A staunch civil libertarian, she argued that a society that permitted and encouraged the free flow of ideas was healthier, smarter, and freer. The Galley ultimately allowed Douglas to

Douglas, second from the left, next to the Miami Public Library's bookmobile, 1940s. Not only did she read broadly and constantly herself, she encouraged others to do so and lent her name and assistance to projects for generating interest in local libraries. Courtesy of Florida State Archives.

play the role of the so-called public intellectual. Yet her columns reveal a depth to her intellectualism that existed far beyond popular newspaper topics.

The passages that follow reflect her intellectual interests. Here she deliberates on books and reading, literature, poetry, film, music, and thought. It was the era of the silent film, and radio broadcasting was just getting off the ground. Reading was still a favorite pastime of Americans. But Douglas seemed to sense the passing of an era, and she used her column to make her loyalty to those activities well known. As far as she was concerned, American culture could benefit from a greater commitment to intellectual pursuits.

Book News in Brief.

Charles M. Schwab, the steel magnate, has just published through Century Company, a little book called "Succeeding With What You Have." In the simplest of English it gives a little well-deserved publicity to the great virtues of honesty, industry and sticking to it. Mr. Schwab promotes the man who does not watch the time clock, who likes his job better than the other man and who has no pretense about him. He believes in men and hard work. The greatest virtue of the book is that it has been written by a man who has done it. Beyond that it is no great splash in the sea of good literature.

(March 7, 1920)

Book News in Brief.

Desperadoes n' Everglades n' Everything.

United States senators who are in charge of Florida land frauds, Seminole Indians, New York toughs, stalwart heroes and beautiful and dauntless heroines, not to mention lots of Florida local color, have been put up in book form by Henry Doyen under the title of "The Plunderers." The result is sufficiently exciting for those who still care for the Desperate Desmond type of fiction. The picture of Everglades land fraud is as accurate as is necessary for the plot and the plot itself moves with unerring rapidity from hand-to-hand fights to love scenes, in quite the accepted manner. As far as the writing goes, it is well enough. The number of fictioneers who write readable English is growing rapidly, demonstrating more and more the need for a growth in mental content to correspond with the improvement in techniques.

But Mr. Doyen has one or two not bad descriptions of Florida scenery.

(March 14, 1920)

With a Yeo-Heave-Ho and a Rum-below.

The National Marine League and the American Library Association ask: What are the ten best books of the sea?

(March 20, 1920)

Our list of sea books, by the way, stands at present in the following order:

Captains Courageous—Kipling.
Typhoon—Conrad.
The Nigger of the Narcissus—Conrad.
Moran—Frank Norris.
Out of Gloucester—James Connolly.
Mr. Midshipman Easy—Captain Marryat.
The Wreck of the Grosvenor—Clarke Russell.
The Sea Wolf—Jack London.

And we should like to include the best of the lot, except that it is poetry, which is John Masefield's "The Story of a Round Hound" otherwise known as "the Dauber."

(March 31, 1920)

Confessions of the Proofreader.

Is it because people think it virtuous to appear to know a lot about music or do people, most people, really know as much about music as they appear to? To the average human being is an excellent piece of violin music, like Elman's the other evening, for instance, any more than a pleasant succession of delightful sounds, or does it have for them a real pattern and a meaning which gives them more than a happy feeling just behind the ears? If this is so, they conceal it well, but still murder will out. For if they have the abilities for a complicated technical enjoyment why did so many people turn to his or her neighbor and hiss, "That's the Ave Maria" at one encore, instead of punctuating the program with more weighty critique and appreciation of themes and andantes and pizzicati and minor movements and things? We must confess that we have our doubts, remembering the thrill of vanity with which we recognized that it was a mute, the thing that he took out of his pocket which made the notes go all thin and eery, like the wind in the tops of ancient willows. That was about as far as our technical knowledge went. But in confessing this, shamefacedly, we also implicate the rest of the audience, who hummed loudly when they recognized the Faust parts in the fantasy. All of us, as lovers of music and cognoscenti, should have hummed and twittered and remarked all the way

through, if we had only known as much as we would like to have other people think we know.

(March 22, 1920)

Book Notes in Brief.

As time goes on the works of Rudyard Kipling are falling into their places in the estimation of the public and of these none hold so high a position, and increasingly so, as *The Jungle Book* and *The Second Jungle Book*. The former has just gone into a fifty-fifth edition while the latter went to press recently for the thirty-ninth time. *The Jungle Books* contain some of the finest writing of the brilliant Anglo-Indian. As a depiction of Indian jungle life they are absolute gospel and for brilliancy and vividness of writing, for clean-cut characterization and for atmosphere they stand without a rival in modern literature. *The Jungle Books* are not for children alone. Only adults can appreciate to the full the jewel-like quality of Kipling's animal masterpieces.

(April 9, 1920)

When anyone says, "You know I really don't have any time to read" I can't help being a little suspicious. Because there is always time for a lot of things, or rather, anything that you want to do badly enough. If you had rather embroider than read, you will embroider. If you had rather play solitaire than read, you will play solitaire. But it isn't the people to whom reading is meat and drink who cannot find time for it.

People are so funny about reading. They are apologetic about it, when they can't find time for it. Or they say, "Now I really have made up my mind to read one book a week," or something like that. Just as if not reading were one of the seven deadly sins but at the same time a temptation which the strongest is liable to.

For people like that books are a task, a penalty, or at least a cultivated gesture, which they, in the secret recesses of their own minds assume only for the purpose of social conquest but never for their own amusement. And it is a constant mystery that people who have that hang-dog attitude about books should ever read anything.

Why, in the name of the nine gods of literature and all common sense, should anyone read if he does not want to? Why must we be bullied into reading as a means of attaining a heavenly crown or anything else, if we do not honestly see any fun in it?

For that is, after all, what books are for. They serve to give those hungry for more life glimpses of that essential commodity in fuller abundance than any individual life is capable. Books do instruct, but even that only if we like them. And why should any one apologize if he does not like a wider experience, a broader panorama of this world, adventures without hazard and treasures without cost? At least, it is not to the world in general he should apologize. It is to himself.

(April 13, 1920)

Confessions of the Galley Slave.

Did you ever realize how the term "high brow" is more and more falling into disrepute as humor? Have you heard anyone recently think an occasional French word funny? Do people still make remarks about consulting a dictionary if you happen to use a longer than two syllable word?

Back in the days of Mark Twain's early efforts it was the height of American humor to mispronounce a name like "Leonardo de Vinci," or not to know that Marcus Aurelius is dead. But is that the idea of the best American wit of today?

Think a minute, and you will realize that the United States is growing less and less ashamed of knowing something. To have read a book, that is no great matter of reproach. To remember Greek with pleasure or ancient history with interest is not nowadays a criminal occurrence. Even in the newspapers of today colloquial translations from Horace are popular. And what would Mark Twain and the primitive American humorist think of the use of French in dress goods advertisements?

No further question, American humor is growing up. Or perhaps Americans are growing educated.

(April 15, 1920)

The Confessions of the Galley Slave.

In celebrating Shakespeare's birthday, someone will be almost sure to mention Bacon, if not in substitution, at least in attempted humor. And that is the ignominy of the Bacon-Shakespeare controversy. It has brought the name of Shakespeare into conjunction with farce, and very poor farce. If it were good farce, rollicking, side-splitting, roistering stuff, then surely the creator of Falstaff and the Sexton and Lear's fool and the other clowns would join in, as hearty as any. But it has the windy, bitter humor of Master Francis Bacon, his wit, and on such a day should be boo'd out of doors.

For the apologists of Bacon base their claims on the pedantic idea that Shakespeare, as yokel, holder of horses, player of minor parts and second-class gentlemen, could never have produced great art.[2] They offer the aristocratic travels, the courtly toadying, the small minded king-following of Lord Verulam in place of the quiet eyes and calm mien of this man Shakespeare. What would he know of Lears and Macbeths who never saw a court? What could he guess of Denmark and Rome, Athens and Bohemia, who knew only the placid curves of the Avon? But they forget that its quiet waters have borne up many a village Ophelia, its banks seen the blindness of many a country Lear, its flowered meads known the pressure of English Titanias and Pucks and its calm pools the reflection of many a questioning and unknown Hamlet.

If Bacon wrote Shakespeare he could not have been Bacon. For Shakespeare, rather than on Roman grandeur, Trojan towers and the far shores of the island of Miranda, looked on the world about him and into his heart and wrote. So did not Bacon, nor any but the few great geniuses who have mirrored this our world.

(April 23, 1920)

The Confessions of the Galley Slave.

On general principles we have always been opposed to censorship of things, on the ground that it does not work in the first place and is never done by people who know anything about it, in the second. But we're converted. We're for a moving picture censorship, a good hard one. But not as you imagine on the moral grounds. The public takes care of that. But what

the movies need is a censorship on the grounds of good taste and vulgarity. We endured a picture last night, that's why. It was made in Miami and, at the risk of getting fired, we're here to state it was cheap, vulgar and criminally unnecessary.

It was one of those supposedly funny ones, where vulgarity takes the place of wit and elaborate fallings over everything take the place of plot. All the old tricks, that were discovered just after the period when they depended on moving trains and runaway horses for interest, were trotted out. There were the comic police, whose humor consist always in looking cross-eyed and falling on each other. There was the comic housemaid who beats the carpet and beats a stray hobo as well. There were the false mustaches that are supposed to be funny since Chaplin invented hirsute humor. There were the stoutish nymphs in curls who hop and skip to register joy. And there was a live snake that had nothing to do with the plot—if there was a plot—which capped the climax that was conspicuous because there wasn't any.

We do not like to think that all the films turned out in Miami are of this caliber, since they are the sort that only young children and the feeble-minded could possibly enjoy. A glimpse or two of a background that might have been lovely if it were not for the inept wiggling and posturing of the actors, are all that stand for Miami publicity.

Perhaps the movie art has to go through these stages before it grows up. But we wonder very heartily if really funny comedies, really original situations and small modicum of grey matter applied to the problem are utterly impossible for Florida? Until then, we're for a censorship that can tell the difference between gymnastics and humor and pointlessness and plot.

(May 16, 1920)

The End of a Perfect Day.

Somebody said the other day, it doesn't matter who, that this Gilbert and Sullivan stuff was much overrated. The songs they're putting out in New York just now are just as good stuff if we only thought so. That may be true, sidestep we, but even Gilbert in his worst moments never wrote words similar to the recent New York hit which begins:

"You may be the world to your mothers
 but
You're a pain in the neck to me."

(May 21, 1920)

Further Difficulties of Colyuming.

At times the filling of this top of column
 Is quickly done, with verses as you've seen,
Of timely interest, not, we hope, too solemn,
 With too much spleen.

But, other days, like this, we find the masthead
 A very cavity, a vacuum,
Our mind for ideas we have fairly blasted
 But none will come.

And yet at rhyming we are fairly clever,
 It isn't metre that makes us frenetic.
Our spondees, dactyls, anapaests forever
 Are energetic.

We know the trick of stringing strophes and couplets,
 Quatrains and ballads, villanelles and odes,
Sonnets and epics, dithyrambs and tercets,
 In several modes.

We like to think that Shakespeare or that Browning
 Like us, lacked ideas on some gloomy day.
We'd write if we, our stubborn Muses frowning,
 Knew what to say.

The Confessions of the Galley Slave.

The difference of attitude some people have about poetry and music is a very curious thing. Music, one of the most difficult of the arts, is to be attempted by anyone, apparently. A single city block will resound with the

strummings and thumpings of half a dozen unfortunate youngsters chained to the parental piano stool by parental admonishings as to the horrors of a musicless future. Phonographs, ukeleles, the human voice sometimes justly called divine, oboes, clarinets and even infantile xylophones, serve to make night noticeable if not melodious. But in how many of these houses and apartments along your block are mothers urging children to read and write poetry?

And yet what is true for one of these arts is true for the other. As children, by the right methods, can be led not only to play with a charming touch but even to improvise, so the fundamental instincts for the right sounding word, the balanced metre, the satisfactory neatness of a well turned rhyme, is perfectly possible to the same children. And how much easier and more valuable for them to read good poetry like "This Battle of Ivry" with its stirring swing, than to stumble through some tinkling and meaningless "Berceuse" or "Valse Caprice" which can give them very little beyond relief that it is over.

We have convinced ourselves that in music lies culture and so we thrust the difficult and tedious art upon unfortunate victims who have no auditory imaginations, and withhold from them the glories of good, mindfilling, sense-satisfying poetry, because, forsooth, poetry has been judged impracticable.

If we looked at this thing rightly, both music and poetry, in the right quantities and from the right attitude, would be available to every child. We would not so much marvel at occasional Opel Whitneys or Hilda Conklings as realize that the normal child can write as well as read, excellent poetry, and in that writing acquires a refuge and an outlet for emotion which, in the long and crowded adult years, would stand them in excellent stead.

(July 3, 1920)

Movie morals are either very black or very white. The good heroine always goes to missionary meetings, gives pennies to beggars and takes large baskets of food to tubercular families who do not believe in race suicide. Bad heroines smoke, dance on tables in hotels, sit on tiger skins and droop a wicked eyelid. If a country girl should go to a cabaret with a city man and take one sip of brownish liquid from a glass, her father in the country will

immediately die and the young man whom she refused to marry will enter just in time to see her do it, with the news. There is no such thing as ordinary morals. Everything goes in the movies but brains. They are absolutely barred.

(July 25, 1920)

An Appeal to Poets.

So often I wonder why poets their thunder
 Throw away on ethereal themes,
When the muse of the kitchen's especially rich in
 Good food for their dreams.

What poetic ardor they'd find in the larder,
 What rapture a roast would reveal,
If they'd once hitch their wagon, in place of a flagon,
 To joys of a meal.

Take an omelette that's yellow, a proper fat fellow,
 With butter discreetly bedight,
And parsley besprinkled with crisp edges crinkled—
 There's rhapsody right.

Or French salad dressing. No subject more pressing.
 No technique of blending more rare,
Than sapphics more skillful, not rash or too willful,
 With consummate care.

I wonder no ballads are written to salads,
 Of lettuce or endive and such,
Or odes to creamed oysters which crude hoi polloi stirs
 With tabasco too much.

What lyrics inspire the taste of pot pie, or
 The fragrance from some fricassees,
Some sonnets to duckling, after Dryden or Suckling,
 I'm anxious to see.

I think it is awful, no lines to a waffle,
 All dripping with syrup and butter,

Have even been printed, though I've often hinted
 Such food is just utterly utter.

Of course there are oodles of things done with noodles
 And brussels sprouts browned in the pan,
And baked ham with spices and raspberry ices,
 All welcome to man.

So poets, hereafter, when prestige and laughter
 You'd seek with the triumphant bays,
For subjects when looking, remember that cooking
 Is worthy of praise.

(August 3, 1920)

An Idea For Ideas.

A verse is not so difficult to write,
It's the thinking up of subjects that I find
Is really most annoying when you've spent an hour toying
With the trivial, trifling contents of your mind.

There are people who can readily provide
Ideas wholesale or in bunches as you like;
But the person with the notion often lacks the locomotion
While the mind that has the method goes on strike.

Or if I had a subject but the tail
For a verse of several inches or for more,
I could leave this yawning Galley for a saunter in the alley,
While the clearing house just matched it from the store.

So if anyone's got ideas for exchange
And needs some rhymes and metres I'll apply—
And between us something cleverer than single heads endeavor
 or
A dozen, we will polish on the fly.

(August 10, 1920)

Lines to the Office Waste Basket.

Wobbly wicker cylinder, yawning from the floor,
 Why gaze on me reproachfully as if I were a bore?
Why swallow all the scraps I feed with such an empty stare;
 Don't you know that people put their masterpieces there?

If you were a friend to me and not a hungry chasm
 You'd treasure all the bits that fall in each creative spasm;
You'd hoard them up till pilgrims came, in reverence and in
 awe,
 To glean the gems of poesy that I feed down your maw.

They say that Mark Twain's wife found half the finest things he
 dreamt
 When he'd thrown them in his own waste basket in
 contempt.
And Milton's daughters picked things out from his scrap
 hamper, too,
 That made him very famous. Now let's see what you can do.

(August 19, 1920)

More Truth Than Poetry About Opinions.

I read two dozen magazines and newspapers each day,
I give a pricked and patient ear to everything they say,
I let them use me as they will to argue or convince,
But then I take me by the hand and give myself these hints.

First, nothing ever is so bad as radicals all shout,
And yet it's always worse than safe conservatives give out,
Because the world's a whole lot bigger than single man,
Or party or profession or church or ring or clan.

And then it's well to notice how many people think
One plan or rule or formula will save us from the brink
Of wild and weird disaster, just one simple little creed,
'Twill renovate, rejuvenate, make perfect, so they plead.

Some think that votes for women or the single tax will do
For men what fifty centuries has proven all too few,
The Simple Life or Thought Force, some religion yet untried,
Will serve to thrust the warring years of futures quite aside.

By taking yeast or buttermilk or going without shoes,
Holding the single standard or rehearsing worn-out views,
Or worshiping the sun or eating uncooked food,
Humanity at once will reach the Only Perfect Good.

So when I've finished all these papers that I read each day,
I marvel at the different things that they have found to say,
And some things are quite weighty and some are very wise,
But if I follow all they say 'twill be a great surprise.

And right here we beg to state to those of our friends who worry about what they are pleased to call our "style" that we know perfectly well that the above is doggerel and not poetry. But then we never said it wasn't.

(August 26, 1920)

Hail, Stars and Stripes.

The one souvenir of the Late War which, more than all others, we would rather have, has just been brought to this office. It is the bound file of the complete issue of the most remarkable newspaper in the history of journalism, THE STARS AND STRIPES, the newspaper carried on by doughboys in France that became the official organ of the A.E.F. [American Expeditionary Force], the only institution that defied all official dictums, placed ability above rank and told the truth about the army always.

We knew many of the men who ran the STARS AND STRIPES in Paris, the editor who was a private soldier, with a first lieutenant for an office boy, who took his authority straight from Washington and who accepted no other jurisdiction, even in the face of possible and threatened court martial, the huge figure of Baldridge, the doughboy artist, whose drawings of the war as published first in this newspaper have become nationally famous and others of that group of first-class newspaper men who were soldiers, young and straight talking and truth seeking.

No description of this file is at all adequate. You have to pore over its crowded pages, as the boys pored over them in the trenches or in detention camps or in rest areas, to realize the wealth that is stored here for future reference, reminiscences and history. No later political vagaries can blur the impression of the war that you get here. No later issues can rob this of the reality. More than the elaborations of writers who toured the front lines and wrote weightily for the *Saturday Evening Post,* more than the statements of generals and visiting congressmen, more than letters home and all the angel cake fiction that was evolved out of it, more than all the books yet unwritten, which will dissect and analyze and resolve the part America played in the war, the STARS AND STRIPES will stand as uncompromising testimony as the French flags in Alsace and the white crosses at Romagne. It is the only thing of its kind in existence.

(August 26, 1920)

Very much has been written about Mark Twain. And even more numerous than the writings are the opinions. The old idea of our national favorite as a crude but whole-souled humorist is gradually giving way to the more rational idea that he was a philosopher and stylist whose best works were neither "The Jumping Frog" nor "A Tramp Abroad." But probably the most significant study of Mark Twain has been made in the recently published volume of Van Wyck Brooks, one of the most brilliant of American literary critics and associate editor of "The Freeman." It is called "The Ordeal of Mark Twain." The most significant fact in the mental make-up of Mark Twain, as we have learned from any of his biographers, notably Albert Bigelow Paine, was an eating pessimism, a sense of thwarted power, a dissatisfaction with his work and with himself which amounted to an obsession.

The statement that Mr. Brooks makes may easily arouse arguments and dissent. And yet he explains this complex of Mark Twain as a result of the warping of his genius to fit the narrow niceties of the Victorian era in which he lived, to curb his exuberant fancy to the gentle restrictions of his wife and his immediate friends, who were certainly harsh critics and we fear, narrow ones. That his genius was of tremendous potentiality any perusal of the unevenness of his words brings out, as well as that he himself never in any way was allowed to approach to that freedom of the artist which, in all other

countries, is considered the very breath in the nostrils of the creative genus. He was a philosopher made to feel his wickedness in not being able to hold to the tenets of the exceedingly orthodox church of the day, to the ideas of his friends, none of them clear-minded enough to recognize that his genius could not be harnessed by their own mental trivialities without affecting it. And finally the book is an indictment of this spirit in all America which is jealous of the fact that the artist rebels against mental standardization, that he must think his own thoughts, whether or not they are the thoughts of the solid citizen of the community, that the whole atmosphere of mental inhibition and intellectual barrenness which America throws up around the creative artist is the one reason why so many of them have to go to Europe for opportunity and audience, or are themselves the product of European ideas in an American setting.

It is a severe indictment, this book of Mr. Brooks. But it's worth all the controversy that is bound to arouse. Indeed, the fact that it will arouse controversy is one of the most encouraging things about it.

(September 16, 1920)

We are informed by someone who has made a study of it, that Woodrow Wilson's favorite word is an adjective. He uses thirty adjectives to one verb. This tendency rather puts him outside the class of great writers whose adjective averages were much lower.[3] With Ruskin the ratio is sixteen verbs to seven adjectives; Carlyle, twelve to four; Macaulay, eleven to three; Poe, twelve to five; Shakespeare, fourteen to nine; Scott, eleven to eight; Dickens, sixteen to six; and Shaw, fourteen to four.

An adjective, we deduce, has fewer resulting political complications and can more easily be reversed.

At the same time, it is the people who use the verb who get things done.

(October 9, 1920)

For Mark Twain's Birthday.

This is your birthday, Mark, not that you care.
Your bitter heart for too long now has lain
Quiet at last with all your hunger healed
And all those wild guffaws and shouted laughter

That followed you are muted in Time's mouth
And all that golden light that through you glowed
In gorgeous phrases, jewelled, many-flowered,
Have held in beauty all the life you caught.
But, bitter heart, our praises cannot show
What aching years, what hot and eating pain
Scourged you, unconscious, to your greatness going.
When in the fullness of your later years
Life fell away and left you there alone
As on the day you gulped your first shrill breath
Was it not truth and beauty you had wrought
That out of years' wrack stark to you remained?

(November 30, 1920)

H. L. Mencken has been for a long time saying that no poetry has ever been
written south of the Mason-Dixon line. Whether he is saying this just to
get a rise out of his readers from the Old South we are not free to testify.
But all we can say is that H. L. Mencken ought to see the contents of our
waste basket. There is a square foot of poetry produced right here in
Florida, which to our knowledge, is still south of the Mason-Dixon line
although of course we have been here only four years and cannot be ex-
pected to know everything. What Mr. Mencken may have been complain-
ing about is that no great poetry has been written in the South. In that case
we should ask Mr. Mencken what he means by great poetry. What we think
he means is that he has read no poetry from the South that makes him cry,
as Lizette Woodworth Reese's sonnet "Tear" does. He hasn't read some of
this stuff. It would make him cry all right. Yet it must be great poetry to
someone or he or she would not send it to us. We confess very little of it
seems great to us, but that is because we have an unalterable prejudice in
favor of the best poetry technique that can be done. This may be wrong in
us. But it is too late to change. We had a Latin woman once who translated
Virgil into English hexameters that marched and sang and were glorious,
no matter what they meant. There was another one later who read Anglo-
Saxon verse until you could hear the wash of the surf on English cliffs and
the tremendous crying of the sea winds over the open wold. We didn't
know what that meant, either, but there was something there on which we

went drunk. So our only rule is, if it doesn't make us drunk its not great poetry to us. And that, after all, is what Mr. Mencken means. He may be right in that the South has produced no great poetry. But it is not because the South does not write it. The trouble is, it writes too much. It overflows in verse on the slightest opportunity. And everybody else sits around and admires it tremendously. It's too easy, that's what writing verse in the South is, too easy. We ought to know. We get away with murder ourselves.

(January 3, 1921)

When the first cave man picked up a flint and scrawled, in the first writing, words on a cliff side, there is little doubt that what he wrote was a remark about himself. And from that time on the supreme interest of man has been in the doings and sayings of himself and his neighbors. In that respect gossip and literature are closely related.

(April 18, 1921)

It's funny how I cannot get "Babbit" out of my mind, in spite of the uncertain feelings it leaves me with. I wonder whether it will be as widely read as "Main Street." It's difficult to say. So many people read "Main Street" out of curiosity and were disgusted with it that perhaps they will not want to adventure with the second one by Sinclair Lewis in the character of holding the mirror up to American life. Yet in every way "Babbit" is a better written book, a more complete picture. And I have a sneaking feeling that the people who would get the maddest at it are the ones who ought to read it. It is undoubtedly a human document, a picture of American life which will take a very important place in the history of American literature. As a parody of the tired business man, it is really a scream.

Where do people get this idea, that free verse is easy to write? I suppose they think rhyming is hard. What was that fight between Ruskin and Whistler, something about Ruskin saying on the stand about Whistler's pictures, that a work of art must show that it was an effort to do. And Whistler's devastating snort that a work of art should never look as if it were hard to do. Something like that. But very apropos. Any child can rhyme or you can buy a rhyming dictionary. Happy thought: What would Walt Whitman have

looked like with a rhyming dictionary? Question: Do I dare spell it "rime," or will they think I don't know how?

(October 2, 1922)

Books, art, the theater, poetry, and the slow growth of the American people into some sort of intelligence, what is there better to talk about? For books, even if it is not the latest, what could be more delightful than Arnold Bennett's latest, "Mr. Prohack," and what a nice thing to contrast with Sinclair Lewis' "Babbitt." For art, goodness, we haven't seen anything but billboards for ages, unless we could talk about gardens, and we're not going to. For theater stuff, there is only the report that Ethel Barrymore is doing some superb acting, and utterly unlike herself, in Hauptmann's "Rose Bernd," the difficult study of a tremendous inarticulate peasant woman. For poetry, well, we've talked about poetry. And for the growth in intelligence of the American people, let's see. Let me see. Well, they don't seem to be much excited over the Turkish question, unless the propaganda begins to come in all about Turkish atrocities and how the Turk ought to be driven out of Europe, but our own lynching record remains about the same and the Congressional Record is still difficult reading. There is one thing though. We haven't been called a highbrow in a week.

(October 3, 1922)

At last we have the complete rejoinder for the word "highbrow," which, used in the deprecatory sense, has often moved us to teeth-gnashing. We have been powerless to ward it off, or to shape an adequate answer which will express us. Until now. And we have not recognized it before. It is the blissful word "moron." If you weren't a highbrow in the old days, you were a lowbrow, and gloried in it. The heights of superiority to which a lowbrow could climb so far have broken all altitude records. Until now. For the devastating thought can occur, if you are not a highbrow, perhaps it is not because you have a divine common sense, but that you are a moron. An awful suspicion, the thought that maybe you simply haven't got the mental muscle. An awful suspicion. But, oh, what a weapon, what a weapon!

The Siasconset School of Opinion at Nantucket has just completed its first summer term and already we are hearing about it. For it was a remark-

able thing. People gathered there, not to organize, not to "do something," but just to think things, to let their minds go vacationing among ideas, not of formulas or dogmas or panaceas, but those old, half-forgotten potent things, ideas. As such. What, oh, right reverends and wrong reverends of every kind, are we coming to? Or is it possible that somebody has remembered that America was founded with the dim idea that freedom to play with ideas was one of the prerequisites of the citizen?

(October 7, 1922)

From a Journalist's Day Book.

Monday, October 16.

Generally I protest bitterly when anyone says, "Goodness, how do you stand the summers in Florida," because the summers don't seem to bother me. But this pre-hurricane weather, if there is to be a hurricane, is a lot more trying. Sunday was one of those days, not so much hot, as reducing one mentally to mush. I sat around all day trying to read Lytton Strachey's "Books and Characters" with some success, and much pleasure in spots, but for the most part miserably conscious of dying of sleepiness, and suddenly waking up, having slept, feeling like a chocolate eclair left out in the sun and then stepped on. It is the first Sunday for years like that that I can remember, with a surrounding flavor of too much peanut candy, too much sleep and complete mental fog. I can remember feeling like that years and years ago, back in Massachusetts. Sunday was always like to be a long gloat of reading, reading anything or everything, it didn't seem to matter what, and even then I could get through three books in a day. But about the late afternoon, having eaten too much Sunday molasses candy, having read too much, with eyes aching and head heavy, I'd feel like this. It takes the advance guard of a hurricane to do it now.

Wednesday, October 18.

I learned with quite a shock the other day that you could actually get symphony music on phonograph records. I don't really know why it should have been such a surprise. Maybe it is because you generally hear nothing but dance music. But since then life has become ten per cent more joyful

because the symphonies that I have heard since on records have been very successful indeed. You get the very picture of all those violin bows rising and moving like a wheat field and you very delightfully miss that whirr and rustle of programme pages that used to be such a nuisance in old Symphony Hall. As a matter of fact, if you can't have a symphony orchestra all to yourself, which is rather difficult these days, I know nothing more delightful than the Schubert Unfinished on a record, and you flat on your back on a couch, soaking it in.

Friday, October 20.

Two hundred books are a drop in the bucket when you come to pick and choose. And yet people are constantly clamoring for a list of ten best books or fifty best books, to make up their library. How can they? The more I try to pick out two hundred, the more I realize that it is impossible to standardize a thing which depends so much on personal needs. Heavens, I could cheerfully make up a library of a thousand and then find a lot the very next day that I simply couldn't wait to read. Maybe that is just as well.

(October 23, 1922)

It is extremely difficult to sit down on an exquisitely lovely November day and compose one line of epigram which will be both crisp and succinct. Not that we have ever done it. But in the moments since we drew the above lines across the paper we have been sitting and thinking that what we needed in this particular space was something preferably short and crisp, something at once profoundly significant and keenly funny. We looked at the clock and saw how little time there was anyway. We looked out the window and rejoiced in a thin mist of cloud low in the sun and as dazzling as a diamond, we looked over our mail again in hopes that we had overlooked something, we scribbled on a piece of paper with a pencil. The exquisitely profound, exquisitely funny line simply was not. It was very much easier, we discovered, to find out what you want than to get it afterward. On the course of our cogitations, however, we did discover that the best things that are said are generally struck off white-hot, apropos of something. You've got to have something to talk about before you say anything; that is, if you want to be brilliant. Running a newspaper column is different. And the more we thought, and remembered brilliant things we had

heard of, the more it seemed to us that the occasion was necessary. Circumstance seems to make wit, just as much as the mental flash that makes it verbal.

(November 20, 1922)

Really, we cannot help thinking that H. G. Wells' latest "Men Like Gods," in, save the mark! Hearst's International, is a very fine piece of work. Whatever one thinks of Mr. Wells, in his constant discovery of some new idea, in his constant giving up of older ideas in favor of the new one, in his smashing productiveness, it seems there is something definitely constructive in this latest. To us, H. G. is always best in the frankly Utopian. That tremendous imaginative power is cramped when he confines it to small unpleasantness like the late war. In the old days, when he was soaring aloft in things like "The War of the Worlds" he really communicated something, a sort of spiritual uplift that will inevitably follow even a brief excursion beyond our ordinary boundaries. And in "Men Like Gods" I am not at all sure that he has not gone beyond his first promise at last. It is a new device for introducing one to a Utopia which he uses, a purely scientific one, smacking, faintly of Einstein and what little an ordinary mortal can know of somebody's lectures on the fourth dimension. But having arrived in his Utopia, Mr. Wells is not only delightfully ingenious, but he is unquestionably big in his vision. He handles some of the ideas which we all feel dimly as somehow important with a serenity, a real beauty, which makes them instantly more real for us. The happy parallel of our times with what the Utopians call "The Age of Confusion," the huge common sense of the Utopian scheme of childbirth, education, government, ownership of property, and the possibilities of the scientific spirit are like a huge window opened in the sky. Just the possibility that the human race may, in some dimly distant age, be anywhere like that, gives a feeling of utter stability to go on which I think, more than anything else, is the need of our present times. The older things in this era of confusion are passing. The new things like the thin sliver of new moon just up from the horizon, give, as yet, very little light. In such times a huge, serene, infinitely confident canvas like this of Mr. Wells is real nourishment for hungry people, starved with shams and untruths and catchwords.

(November 22, 1922)

We have just read a long advice by a soothsayer to a writer, which states that few can hope to write who do not mingle their ink in tears. "A really great writer," we read, "has to suffer before he can feel the emotions he puts on paper." And being as modest as we can, of course, considering everything, we are here to state we know exactly what he means. Tears are mingled with this ink as we write, according to the best formula. We are here to state that we feel, more than feel, the emotions we put in this paper. We have every qualification for being the world's greatest describer of nature. We have suffered, although we are not so sure how strong in our suffering we have become. All we know is that a while ago we came by that corner at the beach where they are building the charming grey house and experienced, for one moment of fleeting agony, what it means to have seen a wall covered with blossoming bougainvillea, before which have been planted the most screaming of red hibiscus. If tears can make a greater writer, we are It.

(December 27, 1922)

I think it is the American newspaper which is a large measure responsible for the curious idea of art which the American people has had. "Has had" because the better newspapers are changing their attitudes, so that at last a little common sense on the question is allowed to seep through to the public. But as a rule the idea is on a newspaper that you cannot possibly criticize anything which a citizen of the locality, or his wife, has done in the way of drama, painting, music or any other art, because he might not like it. Everything has to be superb. Every two by four musician must be another Liszt or another Beethoven. Every small girl who does a dance must be unequaled for her grace and charm. Every small painter or actor must be showered with the superlatives of all adjectives. The idea that the production of the beautiful and complete thing, music, painting, poetry or even a program in a club, is a thing casually to be come by, without the long apprenticeship that is absolutely necessary to any art except that of the phenomenal genius, is a pernicious influence in any community. Under that light everything must be good, and so nothing can be. The greatest can not be distinguished from the less great and we are doomed to a stupid mediocrity which is not only unintelligent, but superlatively sterile. The big city newspapers nowadays employ critics of music who are real critics, book-reviewers who are not afraid to speak plain English, and dramatic critics

who at least are true to their own opinions, if not to others. "But you cannot do that in a small town" is the constant cry of the more timid. Just as if people did not relish a fair and square statement of the truth, and did not respond to it, except when their own toes were stepped on. And if their own toes are stepped on once, and they withdraw their patronage, there is always the possibility that the journal may be so overwhelmingly interesting that their curiosity gets the better of them. To hold up the finest possible standards in art and in thought surely is the province of any newspaper, no matter how feeble. That, it is safe to say, is the only thing the public wants. That it does not always get it serves only to whet its appetite.

(February 1, 1923)

It is quite a liberal education in contemporary literature just to pick up *The Miami Herald* and read the names of the writers now visiting Miami and thinking over what they have written and how they stand in the whole picture of American literature today. Probably one of the most interesting figures in contemporary writing is Ring Lardner, whose writing in the vernacular of baseball and sports and, indeed, of the average American on the street, has gained greater and greater interest. It is undoubtedly true that Mr. Lardner is filling that place in our modern world of letters previously occupied by such truly American figures as Josh Billings, Artemus Ward and Mark Twain in some of his earlier moments. Of course his stuff is funny. It's tremendously funny. But like the others who preceded him Mr. Lardner's stuff is chiefly valuable as a racy (and we mean no pun) vivid picture of contemporary American life, written in the real American language. It is fundamentally American. It has the tang and vigor of original American humor, changed slightly from the older American style of the humor of exaggeration to the more modern method of the humor of sarcasm. Mr. Lardner is as American as Chaucer was English. With no affection toward the writing of formal English, he has evolved a style which we might almost call "regional" considering how much we have used that word. That is, he is interpreting the manners and customs of a particular locality, which is the Main street of America, in the local idiom and in the local tempo. That his picture of American life is slightly exaggerated is only another proof of its value as satire. His style is uncouth because the material from which he takes it is uncouth. We like it, and men like it, because it

presents a true atmosphere. We have very little doubt, personally, that some of Mr. Lardner's will become classic, that it will have a very decided part in the tradition of American letters. He presents more than a human document. He is a real interpreter, whether we like the picture which he presents, or not.

(February 3, 1923)

Nothing could be more fascinating than to be able to listen to a man who has studied intimately, for the purpose of portraiture, the great figures in whose interpretations of the hidden meanings in men's faces has brought him international recognition. Such an artist is Mr. Theodore Spicer-Simson, who is staying briefly in Coconut Grove. His series of bronze medallions of Conrad and Yeats and George Bernard Shaw and Chesterton and Thomas Hardy and W. H. Hudson and dozens of others are to most tremendously interesting studies in character and in personality, aside from the great interest in them as pieces of art. But to hear Mr. Spicer-Simson speak of his subjects from the point of view of the artist-student of character is a revelation. Conrad, for instance. Did you realize that Conrad has the bulk and mass almost of a gorilla, that his skull is shaped massively almost like one, and that he carries his shoulders and arms with the stiff thrust of an old-time sailor? Did you realize that Bernard Shaw's face shows him not as the complete Mephistopheles, but really as a benevolent gentleman, perfectly balanced, keenly intellectual, but kindly? Did you realize that Lord Dunsany's face indicated hauteur and a strong sense of the most complete caste spirit? Would you have thought that Arnold Bennett's mouth was crooked and yet sensitive? You knew that Galsworthy was a typical patrician, but would you have said that his face indicated it so clearly? Or that— but, goodness, one could go on forever playing with the crumbs from Mr. Spicer-Simson's rich table of human interpretations. This is the sort of thing which does not happen to us often, but when it does, should be treasured infinitely.

(February 6, 1923)

The lady who wrote us about Housman's poems interested us very much with the clipping which she sent, but we cannot agree with the reviewer that he is only a minor poet. The last twenty-five years have shown that

"The Shropshire Lad" is very great poetry indeed, not any more minor than lyric verse can be and to our mind only comparable in poignancy with the consummate poet who wrote Ecclesiastes and the poet who translated it into King James English. She asked us what a feminine rhyme meant and evidently confused it with the French, which is different. In English a feminine rhyme occurs when the line ends with an unstressed syllable, a masculine, when the rhymed syllable is the only one. That is a crude way of putting it. It is seen best in this quotation from Housman in which the first and third are feminine rhymes, the second and fourth masculine.

> The lofty shade, advances,
> I fetch my flute and play;
> Come, lads, and learn the dances,
> And praise the tune today.

May we go so far as to recommend to our correspondent, if she is interested in the technique of verse, that the best book we know on the subject is Andrews, "The Reading and Writing of Verse." It is admirable.

(February 7, 1923)

> Poets in Spring.
>
> Poets in love with new words that clatter,
> Spin their thin tinsel in twilight drear,
> Drowning the sounds, with their constant chatter
> Of winds that surge for the dancing year.
> They mourn in the path the petals dying
> Of one wan ivory-pallid rose.
> They forget laughter for sake of sighing,
> A moon that rises, a tide that flows.
>
> For over the year at its crisp young morning
> Where is there sighing in sight of earth?
> With new leaves clean from their dewy morning
> And birds a-bubble with new found mirth.
> Whenever man is, there is cause for sadness,
> By the fool hard hand and the greedy eye.
> But fields forget death in the good March madness

And young leaves glisten and crickets cry.
If I were a poet I'd leave my tower
 Tower of ivory cool and bland,
I would go laughing with grass and flower.
 Lift to the winds to walk hand in hand.
Never a mocker in rapture trilling
 I would not follow with slower call.
Poet, hi, poet, when spring's a-thrilling
Pegasus stamps in his stuffy stall.

We want to call particular attention to the above verse. Thomas Hardy is
a name to be noticed but especially in these recent and rare occasions when
he signs it to poetry. He is not writing very much these days, possibly not
since his tremendous epic the Dynasts, but occasionally does publish a
poem or two. This is quite in contradiction to the critics who believe that a
writer generally begins with verse and develops into novels. Thomas
Hardy's verse, for the most part, has been written since his fame as a novel-
ist had been established. But it is essentially the poetry of maturity, and of
Thomas Hardy's maturity. It is stark, rugged, craggy verse, with little truck-
ling to the smooth flow of words. Like the winds over his own beloved
moors his spirit rather bends his words to his will, like the few rough, bent
trees still harried by the blast on some lonely tor. It is cerebral, rather than
ecstatic poetry which he gives us now, weather beaten, but pithy. And al-
ways memorable.

(March 8, 1923)

William Stanley Braithwaite's magazine anthology for 1922 is out, or rather,
has been out for some time and we have never run across it before yesterday.
It is queer how different years affect its size. The year of the war it was a thin
volume, and very discouraging. But this year it is fat, and fat with good
things, old names, and new ones, packed with many beautiful lines and rich
with a sense of a quickening tradition. Many of the regular stand-bys are
here, Amy Lowell, for instance, with some rhymed studies, and Vachel
Lindsay with "Johnny Appleseed" and H. D. and Henry Bellaman and
Louis Untermyer. But there are new names, too. Kenneth Slade Alling, who
first broke in by way of Don Marquis' column in the *New York Sun,* and

Bernice Lesbia Kenyon, of the "Wellesley group" and many others. One of
the most interesting is Hervey Allen, a nephew of Mrs. A. E. Rickmers. To
us, his poetry is especially fascinating because he is the interpreter of a re-
gion. The rest of the poems in the anthology are for the most part personal
interpretations of the experiences of the individual mood. But with this
whole tremendous and colorful background of American life it seems
strange that more people beside Mr. Allen, Carl Sandburg and Vachel
Lindsay, have not discovered that real originality is a derivative of an honest
and sensitive effort to interpret a people or a place. This is the great value of
Mr. Allen's work and to me a great part of its genuine charm. He has chosen
as his region the country about Charleston, S.C., with all its rich color,
its plaintive minor tones, the character of its people, in short, its whole
meaning, as the purpose of his expression. It seems to me if more young
poets were to set themselves up as the interpreters for their locality, an an-
thology such as this would be a very much greater contribution to Ameri-
can letters.

(March 28, 1923)

It is something interesting to consider what the world would be like, and
what we would all be like, if it were not for fiction. Fiction writers, it is true,
are generally supposed to take their plots and characters from life, or, at
least, to get their inspiration that way. And yet the curious fact is that much
of our modern life derives from fiction. The heroines of fiction walk about
our streets. The heroes of fiction use the same gestures in taking off a hat or
kissing a hand. The glamour of the romantic novel, which is everyone's
ideal, has cast a spell over the world. Not that we care, mind you. This is no
appeal for the suppression of the romantic. Far from it. The ideal lives of
the characters of fiction writers may have had a very great part in shaping
civilization. In fact, I am sure that they have. One can only regret that in
shaping it, they didn't make a better job of it. There is the cult of the
woman, for instance, much more the affair of the early Victorian days than
of ours, who have had to see a war through and no nonsense about it. Way
back in the middle ages, when the knights were crusading in the Holy Land
and the world was a man's world, energetic, coarse, cruel, the cult of the
women grew out of those courts which the wives and mothers of those
knights ruled, and was voiced in the songs and lais of the jongleurs and the

minstrels and the minnesingers, much as the cult of the romantic young man in business is voiced by the *Saturday Evening Post* and the *American*. Love of God, love of king, love of the lady, those were the three devotions emphasized by the equivalent of the fiction writers of the day, and through those three they revolutionized society and made romantic love the glamorous thing it was supposed to be down to the beginning of our century. Whether there is really such a thing as a "grande passion" or not very few people really know. The fiction writers believe it and very many people make a life search for it, such as if they, too, were characters in fiction. But now that the type of our fiction is changing, now that we are going in for grim and very unpleasant reality, now that the only loves celebrated by the modern are unrequited affections, repressions, shattered illusions and all sorts of anatomical what-nots, it will be interesting to see what the reaction on life will be. Personally, we are not in the least worried if that made any difference. It seems to us to be a period of transition, during which time the old ideas of conventional individual happiness through love is rather giving way to a dim idea that there is something finer than that, that the whole development of a people is a more romantic possibility than a secret passion, and that the growth into a knowledge that the mere reproductive emotions of the race are not the most thrilling which it is heir to.

(April 3, 1923)

The *Fort Meyers Tropical* news, printed over in our sister-city to the westward, is a mighty nice little paper and we like to read it because it does catch the feeling of its locality, but when it reproduces a so-called poem of ours without a credit line we feel it our painful necessity to call its attention to the oversight, accident as we are sure that it was. It is our artistic temperament, no doubt, that makes us touchy about these little matters.

(April 18, 1923)

And now comes the newest Utopia of all. I venture to say it will be held as one of the great Utopias and it has come in our day, yours and mine, who are undoubtedly on the threshold of a social recreation. It is H. G. Wells' latest book "Men Like Gods," and it is, no matter how fanciful, a great contribution.

For the thing which Mr. Wells has, which the others, even Edward
Bellamy, had not, is the fact that we are all of us already convinced that in
the next fifty years the control of man over his environment will be tremen-
dously increased. We have learned that there is no end to the power which
the human brain will discover, to be put to the service of mankind. We
have seen the air conquered, and many diseases. We have seen things, im-
possible for centuries, become the toy of today, the force of tomorrow. It is
this huge and only half-guessed power which science has added to man of
which Mr. Wells avails himself. And because we know, as our ancestors did
not, what science can accomplish, we are infinitely more ready to concede
to Mr. Wells that a scientific Utopia such as he pictures is not utterly nor
ultimately impossible.

Through the power which man's knowledge shall wrest from the uni-
verse, Mr. Wells believes, he shall find out how to put down diseases and
make social justice and beautiful abundant lives possible. He calls this age,
through which we are now going, the age of muddle, because we have not
all learned yet that the welfare of humankind can be our only possible in-
terest and aim. When we learn that, Mr. Wells believes, we will find the
means through the possibilities of science. I can imagine no more stimulat-
ing book for us all just now, when the ruin and wreckage of a world utterly
at chaos lies around us, a horrible example, of the misuse of human energy.
Mr. Wells' Utopia may be very much more than two thousand years away,
to his manner of thinking. The more we think about it, the nearer it gets.
Why not Miami, now, as a starter? What's two thousand years, between
friends?

(April 24, 1923)

The latest thing of D. H. Lawrence's "The Captain's Doll" is a mighty sight
more easy reading than anything else of his we've read except "The Lost
Girl." First place, it's three short stories, which helps a lot. In fact, it strikes
us that Mr. Lawrence is much happier with a short story than a long one. A
long one gives his extensive visual imagination too much chance. For con-
trast, we've just re-read "Women in Love" which in spots is tellingly acute
and which gets us completely mixed up, we have to confess it, as to which
woman is which. "The Captain's Doll" is definitely clearer, simpler, more
direct. Then, too, it strikes us that Mr. Lawrence has gotten over some of

his more erratic ideas about sex. Or if he hasn't, he keeps them fairly well hidden in these three. Oh, lots of people won't like them at all. But some of the character work is exceedingly good and some of the descriptions, particularly those of the high Alps, are the most vivid I have ever read. He does that sort of thing very well. The other night, after reading the end of "Women in Love," which is laid in the Alps in winter, I was not only snow blind and snow burned, but chilled to the marrow. It might be a good book for sultry September evenings, next fall.

Just saw a copy of "Rhythmus," the poetry magazine which pays a dollar a line for poetry. Fancy that. The poetry business is looking up. The best market price up to that was ten cents a line and you couldn't always get that. To add to that distinction "Rhythmus" is doing excellent work. It isn't being too wild and erratic, either. Arthur Davison Ficke, for instance, has sold several to "Rhythmus" and he is one of the old school of exact technicians. I remember hearing him argue for two hours, once, about the value of the rhyming couplet at the end of the English sonnet form. So there you are. The return to normalcy; awful word.[4]

(April 26, 1923)

It is quite evident that from various parts of the United States local poets are finding prominence, who, each one, are valuable not only because they are for their region. We need such region interpreters in the United States, we need them badly. We must have a deepening sense of the immediate beauty and romance of our own surroundings, we need the interpretations which all forms of art can give to the settings of our ordinary lives. It is a period when America must turn to itself, to its own backgrounds, for beauty and significance. Carl Sandburg has done it for Chicago, Edgar Lee Masters for the middle west, Robert Frost for New England, among others. One of the most recent groups are the two poets who publish, under the title of "Carolina Chansons," their own interpretations of the Carolinas, and especially Charleston, with its wealth of mellow memories.

(May 7, 1923)

And what applies to cookery, which is a very great art and not by any woman to be despised, applies to everything else. People talk about Long-

fellow as a great poet, when he was only a fourth-rate one, and do not know anything about modern poets such as Robert Frost and Vachel Lindsay. People are not satisfied with mediocre books like those of A. S. M. Hutchinson or Colingby Dawson when the really great things of the world, all the time, are on the same shelves for them to enjoy. They seem to be afraid of the best, even when they know what it is.

(May 28, 1923)

It is pleasant to think that people are being interested in that most delightful of American documents "Forty Years Recollections by P. T. Barnum." I don't know who has resurrected it, but some enterprising publisher has reprinted it, with, I hope, the original steel engravings of the first Barnum Museum in Ann street, with the hand painting of strange snakes and animals between the windows, the reproductions of Jenny Lind's playbills, and the picture of the elephant plowing good Connecticut mud with a trainload of amazed passengers trundling by on the wood burning railroad behind. Don't ask me where you can get this book now. I don't need a copy to remember it. The very book reviews conjure up the smells of a black walnut early-Victorian bookcase in what was known as the "writing room" in which nobody ever wrote, where were also many fat pre–Civil War volumes in faded calf, an early set of Dickens, a "History of the Great Rebellion," "A History of the Johnstown Flood" and three black bound "Reports of the Secretary of Agriculture for 1881," which were very dry reading indeed and only to be resorted to in an extremity. But Barnum, bless his heart, was one of the joys of the world. Not even Huckleberry Finn could be more American than this fascinating autobiography of the shrewd old showman who first developed the great American art of advertising but who was first to discover that the American people admire a man who is smart enough to swindle them and tell them about it afterward. Nobody ever wrote a novel that is more typical of early America than this. You find a reality to it which is not in "The Rose of Silas Lapham" or any English attempt at dissecting that strange compound of child and braggart and conqueror, swindler and dreamer, which was the first generation after the pioneer, and funny—oh, goodness. But most of all now utterly lovable. Really, the more I think of it, the "Forty Years Recollection of P. T.

Barnum" is one of the great American classics and should be so considered. And goodness knows that man could write.

(June 15, 1923)

Mr. George Och-Oakes says that rather than see the works of H. G. Wells, May Sinclair, Edgar Lee Masters, Sherwood Anderson, Ben Hecht, and Joseph Hergesheimer in the hands of his two sons he would prefer to see morphine and a loaded pistol in their possession, says a news item, and somehow we cannot help feeling that the sons of Mr. George Och-Oakes, no matter what their ages, rather than be the sons of Mr. George Och-Oakes would prefer to be the sons of H. G. Wells, May Sinclair, Edgar Lee Masters, Sherwood Anderson, Ben Hecht or Joseph Hergesheimer.

(June 16, 1923)

Of course we are perfectly aware that the more worries a person has the less he has time to worry about being a person, like the dog and the fleas, but at the same time we wished to be excused just now for adding to our list of worries that one about the immediate and terrible necessity for grand opera to be sung in English. At that point, we start in to be brave.

(June 22, 1923)

᧑ 7 ᧑ Philosopher and Observer
of Human Nature

Douglas had much to say about the affairs of daily living. Her enunciations were shaped by a strong set of continually developing personal views about how to experience life. She believed in living frugally and simply, perhaps because she never had much money. Friendships to her were the real measure of wealth and self-fulfillment; yet she was capable of being jaded. Life's reward was not always happiness, she knew, and beyond friends and family, one was alone in an indifferent world. In one of the selections offered in this chapter, she called for "a little wholesale gloom" in a world that was artificially cheery.

She also saw religion as artificial. She believed in no world or reality beyond the physical, except that of the human imagination. Her 1923 poem "A Brief Outline of the History of Heaven," included below, suggests her doubts. She was, nevertheless, a spiritual person, according to those who knew her. She approached life as an explorer and inquirer and it was in knowledge gained by pursuing it through personal experience and education and then by possessing it within one's inner self that she found the animating force of life. She did not believe in living by a fixed philosophy but by "working our way through life, trying to learn what makes sense and what doesn't."[1]

If she did not share her beliefs openly with her readers, her columns frequently hinted at them. Her words were reflective rather than preachy; she was Rodin's *Thinker* in newspaper print. When at Wellesley, she recalled, what lay at the center of human existence was drilled into the students.

It was thought, whether of stars or poetry or planets, of molecules or glaciers, winds, acids, stones, the English novel, languages, whether by words or formulae or equations which had stimulated the limitless possibilities of the human imagination and tested the realities of human reason. We were urged to understand that the single great achievement in our own lives must be thought, without which no human act was possible or experience valid.[2]

In the following selections, Douglas touches on religion, money, personal habits, and daily existence. Hers was often a folksy, entertaining sort of philosophy cast in the form of humorous maxims. But in understanding

Sometime around 1947, publication year of *The Everglades: River of Grass.* Douglas's outgoing personality and love of fun never kept her from analyzing human life with serious intent, and she often shared her homespun philosophy with readers of The Galley. Courtesy of Florida State Archives.

Douglas's wit, one also understands that her beliefs were neither facile nor conveyed through humor simply for humor's sake.

And then again, you should say to yourself every night before retiring. "To-day, have I, or have I not, really evocated a nuance?"

(April 2, 1920)

The Confessions of the Proofreader.

In the face of all this sunny and cheerful literature, from "Pollyanna" to "Smilin' Through," it seems to me that what this world needs today is a little wholesale gloom. Let's have a Gloom Club. Let's get together and dare to be pessimistic. Let's publicly annihilate the person who is always telling us to Cheer Up, to Keep Bright, to Look on the Bright Side, to Believe in the Best.

Let's cultivate a good, thorough sane grouch, for a rest and a change.

This is Blue Monday.

Things are in an awful way.

We don't know who is going to be the next president and we don't really know what we are as long as we can make both ends touch.

The high cost of diamonds and white kid shoes and pate de foie gras and permanent waves and satin bathing suits will probably continue to soar.

It will be hot in August down here and because more people than ever are staying down for the summer we won't have any room or any peace and quiet.

They'll build so many houses this summer that we won't be able to sleep in the daytime.

Maybe some mosquitoes will get through that hole in the screen porch and life will be miserable.

The trade winds will only blow between 9 o'clock and sundown and you can't keep your papers on your desk if they do.

The only kinds of meat you can buy in this town are beef, pork, veal, mutton, chicken and canned tuna fish, so we'll probably die of monotony.

Now that they've taken away the wood block paving from Twelfth street the rainy season won't be any fun any more.

Somebody is sure to build a skyscraper or something next to us so that we won't be able to see the airplanes any more.

All the people who have just gone away said they were coming back next year and with all the new ones that will come beside what in the name of time are we going to do with all those people?

Guess Miami's a pretty poor sort of a town anyway. It didn't have sense enough to stay a village but it had to grow up over night. And just look at the darn thing now.

You can't throw a line off the causeway without getting a bite, somebody's always trying to give you money for that lot you bought for nothing three years ago and if the business in this town keeps on the way it's begun, some day we'll have to pay an income tax.

It's awful.

(April 5, 1920)

Speaking of profiteers, we have to agree with Cervantes that every man is as God made him and often times a great deal worse.

(April 9, 1920)

I sing the value of impatience. It is a good vice, if rightly applied. I would be impatient with much, that much more would result, rather than follow the councils of the optimistic and the too-tolerant who believe that in patience all things are accomplished.

Let us be impatient. Let us be impatient about sham things, such as artistic temperament in those who are not great artists, slip-shod work in those who declare they are above work and above all with sentimentalities from those who are too mentally lazy to reason.

Let us be impatient with all bunk, of all kinds, bunk that is given us by people who would be thought socially superior or unusually blue-blooded or unjustifiably aristocratic, bunk that is exuded by those who are not honest with themselves or above everything have so atrophied their powers of observation that they can no longer see themselves as they should.

Let us be impatient with substitute thought for those who never think, substitute wisdom from those who are not wise, substitute ideas from those who have not the courage to create their own.

With such shams, substitutes, mental tricksters, bunk, formulas, second rate opinions, second handed reasons, let us rejoice to be impatient, putting ourselves, of course, at the head of the list.

(April 12, 1920)

Nowadays, one half the world does not know how the other half lives, and can't even guess.

(April 23, 1920)

Persons We Have No Desire To Meet.

The yokel who first circulated the rumor that the efficient person gets up early.

A cynic, speaking of nothing at all, is a man who is very bitter about something which is not quite true.

(April 24, 1920)

Our own suggestion would be to name the streets after real estate agents. The streets should be the ones that get you going and the avenues the ones that get you coming. And Twelfth street could be a Neutral street with all real estate agents barred. Then no matter where you were you'd know where you were.

(May 9, 1920)

The Ouija Board.
In spite of troublous times and problems many
 Of politics and peace and Turkish hordes,
We've left our jobs and golf and thoughts, if any,
 To work the ouija board.

Around our heads the spirits, buzzing daily,
 Direct our lives, vote, write, and keep us floored.
No act of ours is wise unless we, daily,
 Consult the ouija board.

> And yet, perhaps, when this cheap fad is over
> When common sense is partially restored,
> We'll have the nerve to let ourselves discover
> We were the ouija bored.

(May 14, 1920; reprinted in the New York Sun, *June 1, 1920)*

The Confessions of the Galley Slave.

Because the sun has come out again and because we have just had a shampoo and because our new heels make us feel pretty spry we are taking courage to be heretical about several things, which we admit should be approached as a rule with bated breath.

These things we believe, as opposed to current faith—

1. That Mary Pickford cannot act. All she has is curls and cute legs and a reputation.
2. That the public knows a lot more than it is generally given credit for.
3. That the poems of Ella Wheeler Wilcox are not worth the paper they are printed on.
4. That half of Paderewski's reputation as a pianist depended on his hands and his stage lighting.
5. That Harold Bell Wright's success is a result of nothing more than an avalanche of publicity.
6. That popular musical taste is bounded on the north by Handel's "Largo," on the south by that thing the musician of the graduating class plays of Rachmaninoff, on the east by "The End of a Perfect Day" and on the west by "You'd Be Surprised."
7. That the average citizen is ashamed of being caught reading.
8. That the most unusual thing under the sun is individual thinking.
9. That finger bowls are not essentially humorous.
10. That any one who says, "like" instead of "as," "as for instance," "the balance" for "the rest" or who says "different than" in place of "different from" can never be suspected of having had an education.

(May 22, 1920)

Our idea of complete illiteracy is the man who cannot read his own mind.

(May 27, 1920)

The philosophers who say that the imagination is only a deformation of
the memory surely would not have us believe that the authors of some of
those hair-raising episodes in the movies ever lived through them—or half
forgot them.

(May 29, 1920)

The Confessions of a Galley Slave.

In a few cities throughout our rather perplexing country the word "culture"
is feebly beginning to lift its head. Struck down by the perversions of the
German "kultur," subordinated to the hard needs of the war, crushed by
the wave of new rich, the yearning for material luxuries, since the war, the
old quality called culture was practically forgotten. Books have given place
to publicity and advertising, good music was forgotten for expensive cloth-
ing, and the demands of the newly enriched proletariat for unnecessary
furs, silver and jewelry, in place of those qualities of the mind one termed
genuinely aristocratic, seemed for a while to be the only demands which
the country regarded. But perhaps that is changing. In one or two maga-
zine articles recently the word "culture" has been seen. True, it was a hidden
and shamefaced subject, but at least it was there. It was remembered that
culture was once the search for the "best that was known and thought in
the world." Somewhere else someone has dared to mention the fact that a
little more culture and a little less commercialism would make us happier
and perhaps worthier beings. The statement risks being drowned out by a
flood of scorn from those who can see in "culture" no monetary value. The
road to it was always hard, it meant mental activity. Therefore it was worth-
less. But it still exists. We have seen it somewhere. Can it be morning, or
only false dawn?

(May 31, 1920)

We are inclining to the belief that a census of heaven would also show the
population much less than some people think.

(June 15, 1920)

Love is generally considered to be something very much like our late army, everybody who was out wanted to get in and everybody who was in longed for the time when he could be out.

(June 25, 1920)

The Confessions of the Galley Slave.

I must confess that I have a free conscience about this. No one asked me to confess it. I was under no force or compulsion or apparent necessity. But confessions are often like that. We are impelled to them, not by say outward manifestation, individual or social or both, not by some cosmic urge or proportions sufficient to overcome our inhibited reticence, not even by the pin prick of a jaded conscience. No, not for any of those reasons, sufficient as they are, can I make this. I can only say, revealing helplessly and shamelessly the power which actuates my deeds, even the most shameful, that the only reason or, if you prefer, explanation, for my having written the above, with its ratiocinations and adumbrations, is that I needed just about two inches with which to fill up the colyum.

(July 1, 1920)

This is the blessed time of year when the newspaper jokester has a comparatively easy time of it. In addition to the two conventions and the League of Nations there is the one-piece bathing suit, the profiteer, watermelons, corn on the cob, prohibition and mosquitoes. Tell me what a country laughs at and I'll tell you what it is.

(July 2, 1920)

The latest reason for the high cost of everything is that they are making moonshine out of it, including lumber and naval stores.

(July 29, 1920)

Two cent stamps are still being sold for two cents but somehow we don't get the same two cents worth of delivery.

(August 11, 1920)

The race may not always be to the swift, but if it isn't we've always had a suspicion that there must be something wrong somewhere.

(August 12, 1920)

It is a curious thing that some of the tourists who are now flocking to the battlefields in France did not take advantage of the excellent excursion rates offered by the government a year or two ago.

(August 14, 1920)

The more one sees of life the more one realizes that the humorists are the only true philosophers.

(August 15, 1920)

It is a wise man who knows his own home brew.

(August 16, 1920)

We have also a proposition on for secretly selling out the whole middle of the Galley for an advertisement and then leaving for our vacation on the proceeds the morning the ad. is published. We need the money. Probably there are many energetic advertisers who are this moment sobbing and wringing their hands for the space. So everybody would be happy but the business department and who cares for the business department except on Fridays?

(August 17, 1920)

A Letter From Gustavas Adolphus.

Dear galley slave well galley slave here we are on our vacation having a luvly time wish you were here with us yesterday johnny the next to youngest fell out of the window and this morning mrs. adolphus came near being taken in by a cat she hadnt been properly introduced to and just now i got a stiff leg from not dodging in time when a man threw a brick at me but then what can you expect on a vacation it will make us appreciate home all the

more thats what i always say look on the bright side i see by the paper where
the price of cheese is going up now galley slave are you going to stand for
this kind of thing its robbry and if the cheese trust that is working its
nafaryious practices on we poor honest hardworkin mice don't stop pretty
soon the mice of this great and gloryious country will stop eating cheese
and then what will they do what will they hey ask them that if you dare to
speak out honestly for once in a way yrs respectively
gustavas adolphus

(August 27, 1920)

For the truth of the matter is that we are all kept in one way or another. A
perfectly disinterested man does not exist. If he did, he would not be recog-
nized as a man but as a monstrosity. There is no such thing as a disinter-
ested argument, or it would not be an argument at all, since the object of
any argument is to convince others to your way of thinking, no matter for
what reason we think it.

For in spite of all our idealism and the mass of words and phrases with
which we like to dress up our conception of ourselves, the human race has
not yet gone beyond the control of the three fundamental necessities, for
life, for food, for the propagation and protection of the next generation. It
is no good being shocked at the idea that these three control and color all
our opinions, any more than it is reasonable to be shocked at the idea that
man has two legs. The most superficial intelligence will see at a glance this
is true.

Everything in our lives wraps itself around these necessities. Art and lit-
erature are only a means by which we seem mentally to gain for ourselves
pleasanter life than we are actually living. It is the craving for life that
makes us struggle against threatened death, that makes us seek more expe-
rience, more adventures, that unconsciously makes youth rebel against set
forms. And it is a curious statement, but I am of the opinion that even
suicide is a result of this craving for a painless existence, since to the suicide
it is the painful existing world that is wiped out and eliminated, rather than
the person himself. We love day dreaming and dime novels and the movies
because they make us think that life is as we want it to be, thoroughly
painless.

And every one of our opinions, to go back a long way, is colored and influenced by these three. You can't convince a coal miner trying to support seven children on a small salary that there is anything good at all in the idea of capitalism, which to him is merely a bloated monster who has robbed his children. You can't convince capital harried by taxes and trying to do business under constant national persecution that labor is anything but a disintegrating menace, to be fought with the same primitive weapons that the miner would use. Neither one nor the other of these opinions is more moral or ethical or better than the other, since they are made of the same thing.

In these conflicting opinions by which we are so bewildered today, therefore, these three necessities are the only sure guides and fundamentals. No one man or group is freer than another. They are only more or less clever at concealing them, more or less clever in adapting their abilities to get them. Every one is controlled by them, the most intelligent as well as the most primitive.

That is why those who lift their voices and whine the most bitterly are generally the weaker, using another method for gaining what they want. But they are not doing it out of a disinterested love of mankind in general, but because their own three fundamental necessities are at stake. Sentimentality, idealism and all the beliefs of mankind are a mental refuge from the pain of this primitive encounter. It is the urge behind the attacker as well as the attacked.

(September 2, 1920)

The necessity for food makes us make war. It would get the most civilized men in the world fighting for it, if not enough existed. It made the struggle for existence, which made evolution and produced this so-called intelligence of which we are so vain.

(September 6, 1920)

It is a safe bet that some nice motherly women are already making arrangements to have a constitutional amendment to prohibit automobiles from crashing into trucks loaded with T.N.T. in Wall Street.

Or else maybe it serves the people right who were in Wall Street, anyway. Dreadful place. They're regular gamblers, my dear.

(September 17, 1920)

An egoist is a person who thinks he is the most important person on earth, when all the time you know you are.

Sometimes it is safer to judge a man by what he wears because there is so little under it.

(September 18, 1920)

It is obvious that none of us can be strong enough to live without refuges. Whether it is from wickedness of the world or the high cost of living or from a sense of inferiority, we all, at one time or another, seek shelter. And that shelter may be the movies or drink or a new religion or an old book; invariably, saint, sinner, materialist, business man or upholder of the League of Nations, it catches us unawares. Hobbies are such refuges and fine theories of government and the contemplation of all beauty such as sunsets or great music or poetry. But it is obvious, therefore, that, since we must seek refuge from time to time, it is a worthier and more sensible thing to seek those things which open out windows for our minds, rather than those which throw fetters about our bodies. Such is the value of great books, of true books stripped of sentimentality, stripped, perhaps, to the mere granite of existence, but which, by opening new avenues of experience, are the greatest refuges from those experiences which already hem us in too closely.

(September 23, 1920)

Many people believe that any faith is good so long as it makes people better. They make their mistakes in not recognizing that what makes them better may make others worse.

(October 1, 1920)

We have seen, and made, many statements about the real difficulties of colyuming. Here is the real one: Thinking up a last line.

(October 11, 1920)

Idealism is one of the supreme emotions most truly felt in complete isolation.

(December 8, 1920)

It is a curious thing to reflect that the men who are good at figures do not pick the best-looking wives.

(January 18, 1921)

Truth may be stranger than fiction, but most people still cling to fiction. It is more amenable.

(April 4, 1921)

At last we have found out what the theory of relativity is. Professor Einstein says: "Relativity relinquishes the absoluteness of simultaneity." Thank goodness, that's over.

(May 2, 1921)

We would not wish to conceal for a moment the fact that at times we consider running a column very much like walking a tight rope. The tight-rope simile is good, for very many reasons, but especially so on the point of humor. Ever since the Top Guy told us we are supposed to be humorous, we've taken it very seriously. For, after all, what is humor? We don't know. We think it is something that makes us laugh; but the trouble is, that we laugh at a good many things, not all of which other people consider comic. Then, again, we have seen people splitting their sides, and rolling on the floor, and all that, just as we are giving an excellent imitation of a man being arrested for murder. Of course, if our sense of humor were a private affair, it would be all right. We could go up in our room and shut the shut-

ters and have a lovely and humorous time being as funny as we saw fit. But in a column, one's sense of humor gets all the privacy of the w. k. goldfish. So it gets self-conscious and goes running all over the place, retrieving bits of humor and bringing them back wistful and wagging and hoping that some one will stoop over and say, "Good dog."

For instance, there's the question of prohibition. Now, to tell the honest-to-goodness truth, we don't care so awfully much one way or the other. In general, we think the principle is wrong; but the practice doesn't worry us. But, on the other hand, you couldn't run a column two days without anti-prohibition booze. Booze to a column is just like tea to the English.

Then, again, we don't think short skirts are funny. On the contrary, we think they are extremely sensible. But you can't run a funny column on mere sense, you know. It simply isn't done. Sense in a column of alleged humor is like a cup of tea in a melodrama. But we make jokes like "A lot to show for a $9 silk stocking," just because we hope that some one will think that funny, even if we don't get so awfully excited about it.

For, as a matter of fact, the kind of humor we really enjoy in the semi-privacy of our American castle is more this sort of thing: Oscar Wilde said, "I have known men come to London full of bright prospects and seen them complete wrecks in a few months through a habit of answering letters." Now, we really like that sort of thing; we really do. Of course, maybe it is because we never answer our letters, either. But, at any rate, do you or don't you snatch at our meaning—that humor is like meat? It may poison some-body else's dog. In the words of Archie, "Is it or is it not a ball of fire?" It is a ball of fire.[3]

(May 29, 1921)

It is a curious thing to contemplate that no thing is ever declared moral until it is subscribed to by the will of the majority. Before then the greatest righteousness of conduct, no matter how admirable, cannot seem to stand alone. Yet they say truth is absolute.

(December 23, 1921)

This getting up early is always a mystery to me. People make such a fetish of it. I suppose, if you have a lot to do, and it begins early in the morning,

that it is well to get up and be at it, if you can. But why the fact of getting up early makes one more righteous than if one slept peacefully until later is not clearly revealed. When I get up early, which I can always do on extraordinary occasions, but never on ordinary ones, I never feel righteous, but groggy or thrilled, depending entirely on the size of the adventure to be encountered. I remembered once—but goodness, getting up early in the morning, as early as two or three or four, brings very many things to remember.

(October 23, 1922)

Epigram.
We cried to the Lord that He might shatter His handiwork
And do it over again better.
But the Lord said to us: "Fix it up to suit yourselves.
I'm tired of your complaining. I make you a present of it."
Whereupon we have all turned optimists,
Determined, out of sheer laziness,
That this is the best of all possible worlds.

(October 24, 1922)

From the Day Book of a Journalist.

Monday, 6 November.

It has always seemed to me strange that people seem so afraid of being alone. I think it was Maeterlinck who said that people are afraid of silence, which is somewhat the same thing. I have heard people say they did not like long railway trips, because it "made them think too much." And people are constantly asking you if you are not lonely, if they catch you staring out of the window in a room to yourself, or doing nothing at an empty desk in an emptier office.

Yet what, really, are they afraid of? Is it themselves who bore them? Have they no tranquility within them, no inner resource for enriching times when they cannot be talking to people? Or are they afraid to face themselves, to find out really how valuable are some of the things they are always

saying, or how substantial are the things which they are giving their lives to get? It always seems to me that the deepest satisfaction that life can give lies for the individual in those moments of quiet calm, of almost dreaming, when in a flash one really savors reality. It is as if suddenly the life of the past and of the future, in which we spend so much time, were stripped away, and there were left only the immutable present, in which the only necessity was to breathe deep of living, itself, the sheer state of existing. I think such moments generally come when one is looking out of a window, or is out of doors, unless it is by an open fire with a book and a kitten purring. The wind comes soft and still. There is an insect, or a sawmill, buzzing away in the distance, and perhaps there are uncertain noises, traffic noises, or birds, of the quiet. But it is the clear outline of reality, the sheer beauty of leaves, glittering in the sun, a gleam of river, a cloud, a bit of green grass, and yourself tingling to living, not going to live, or having lived, but living, that is the joyous and satisfying thing. To describe such deep moments of well savored reality is to spoil them. One can hardly be conscious of them, hardly phrase them, even mentally. But I am very sure that children know them often, and wise people and the kind who never grow old, because there is no passing, exactly, of this great stream of being, but only a deeper and deeper gusto for it, and with it, and because of it. One is never alone, then, but only a cell in the tremendous [web] of life going somewhere, being something, being itself.

(November 13, 1922)

There is no delight like being able to read on a quiet porch, shaded by vines, and look up from one's book to a view that reaches as far as the horizon. It is a constant thrill to me to be able to do so. Yesterday the view lay across a gentle slope to the bay; across tall grass and flowering weeds fragrant in the sun; across a tangle of weedy growths, and past the fountains of glitter which were palm trees in the sun, and so out across the blue, bright waters of the bay to the faint clear line of Cape Florida and the outer sea, and so at last to the sky. That long reach of vision is a lifting up, a lifting out, mentally as well as visually, and I am beginning to believe that such liftings out have a real effect on one's inner life; and I hope a permanent one. Nothing could be more delightful than to be absorbed into reading which is close and concentrated, and then be able to look up and out, satu-

rating one's eyes with distance. It is a sort of physical confirmation of one's belief that thought will more and more be lifted up and out, as one's gaze is. Certainly there must be some such idea behind our use of the word "vision" to mean, not just seeing with the eye, but a sort of plunge and fright of the mind, which can distance everything but time, and which makes very little of that. And to let one's gaze roam the seven miles or so which it is allowed to the horizon, and then let one's mind, like an airplane taking off, reach out from that, and around the earth and back in forty winks, is surely one of the pleasures which man has and which the animals have not. That is the reason why it is right that we should recognize the tremendous force that the imagination is. And why fairy books are excellent mental gymnastics.

(November 21, 1922)

A Chant for a Thousand Years.

Where were ivory cities
In the days of the world when the slime still stirred?
Where were the hope of race, people walking proudly upright?
Only the slime and the life of the slime was there,
Only the morning of great things for the slime.
For the slime stirring in the new of the world.

On what proud pinnacle do you stand, O man,
That you are scornful of the slime?
Out of the slime by infinite ages you have come.
Are you perfect? Is any man perfect?
Let you remember the slime stirring in the new of the old
 world.

On what proud pinnacle do you stand, oh man,
In you are there no dreams stirring?
Is the upward way ended and over?
Is the morning night?
Let you remember the slime stirring in the new of the world.

Do you dream in secret of a noble people?
Let you remember the slime.

Within you also there is a thing stirring;
Within you, the perfect association;
Within you the wise and beautiful nation;
Within you the nation which shall make one over the earth.
Even now this thing stirs within you,
Stirs in your longings, stirs in your secret dreams,
Stirs in you mightily, the mighty age which is to come.
Even as you, O man,
Stirred in the slime stirring in the new of the world.

We are heartily in agreement with the ideas of our correspondent that we need "an open door to real conversation and an intelligent exchange of ideas." We do need such a medium badly. There is no such thing, really, in our common life here together. The newspapers are not, the churches are not, apparently the Woman's club is not to be allowed to be. Unless one takes to a soap box in the park, a very stupid method, there is really no means at all by which the people can get together and talk about ideas. We differ from our correspondent, however, that a salon, in the old French manner, is the ideal method. After all, a salon and a drawing room mean the interchange of ideas of a little group of people, moving in the same orbit, actuated by the same ends, cursed with that terrible curse, polite society. We do not think that a salon would be the thing, because in the first place we do not think that it would really give the right atmosphere here, where everybody has access to ideas, if he can only get the social contacts which will stimulate him into thinking about them. What we do need, and we have said it before and we will probably say it again, is a real open forum, a place where everybody who likes to can come and discuss everything, as they do in Boston or in dozens of other forward-looking cities. The right atmosphere of a forum is like the old town meeting, a place of real freedom for the people of any town, where, under the courteous, intelligent technique of a forum, the steel of mind can really sharpen itself on the steel of other minds, and where a fine intelligent audience can make friends with itself. That is what Miami needs badly. We understand that the Realty Board is to sponsor one later in December. We could use it right now.

(November 22, 1922)

Nothing could be more chaotic than the period through which we have been going. Mob psychology has clutched us all at one time or another in the last ten years. We have gone at the heels of this and that new tendency, for one reason or the other, and out of a profound disillusionment we have turned more and more to individual prestige and importance, with ourselves as the preferred individual, because we could see very little in the welter of varying opinions about us in which to believe, in which to pin any sort of faith. Yet if we stop and look at the last sixty or seventy years, as Havelock Ellis has done in this book of his [*The New Spirit*] which we are talking about, we may see that the seeds of a great change have put forth little green shoots. Renascence has come before, says Mr. Ellis, and he means a great wind of new vitality, of new intelligence, of great collective emotion, which has made over people and nations and eras. "There is now renascence of the human spirit unless some mighty leverage has been at work long previously. Such forces work underground, slowly and coarsely and patiently, during barren periods, and they meet with such contempt as destructive of man's finer and higher nature; but, in the end, it is by these that the finer and higher nature is lifted to new levels. No great spiritual eruption can take place without the aid of such levers."

The time is ripe for a new birth, for a genuine renascence. Just as the rediscovery of Greek thought brought the Italian renascence, or the discovery of the new world brought the Elizabethan renascence, so during the last century there have been three forces slowly and tremendously working to produce a greater one.

The first force was the evolutionary concept of Darwin—of the immense value of this Havelock Ellis says, "Man has been brought into line with the rest of life; a mysterious chasm has been filled up; a few fruitful hints have been received which help to make the development of all life more intelligible."

Real education and reasonable social organization, these are the only possible bases for democracy. Through what great figures that spirit and these ideas have been transmitted we shall see tomorrow.

(November 23, 1922)

A Brief Outline for the History of Heaven.

I would write if I could, the history of heaven.
Heaven that man has built out of his longings,
That he has peopled with dim gods.
Out of the slime struggling he has built his heaven.
If only for surcease of struggling.
In the vast forecast he built his heaven,
Crouching about some smoky camp fire
Fearful of fear in the dark and the sudden pounce of nameless
 things.
On the shore of the unknown sea where he stood shivering he
 built his heaven
As rest and release from the terrible menace of the cold waves
Out of battles he built glorious heavens for warriors,
Out of soil and of dark and of hunger he built heavens of
 warmth, of his nature
And furnished them forth with the gold and the silver, the
 sapphire and crystal and ebony,
The scarlet and the brass, the pomps and the glory of all his
 desires.
Weak and cold and afraid he built him impossible grandeurs
Tortured and miserable he constructed release in impossible
 joyousness.
And he died, every man of him, and went where we do not
 know.
Behind him the heavens which he has discarded are a mist of
 dreams.
From heaven to heaven he has come slowly, building and
 building in the night time, in the moments before sleep,
Building new heavens when the old heavens have failed him,
Building a new heaven always to fit a new agony,
But now in the new day has come a change in his heavens;
There is a new feeling in him.
There is a new feeling in his heavens.
He has grown tall and strong and the machines he has made
 are new weapons on his right hand and on his left

In his timidity he no longer builds heavens.
He is standing up and gazing about him with calm eyes.
He is forgetting to be afraid.
He is looking at the cities which he built while he was thinking
 of heavens.
He is saying, "What city is this but the city of heaven?"
He is looking at people and saying,
"What people are these but the citizens of heaven?"
Out of his old longing and his forgotten heavens man is a new
 thing.
His heavens are too weak for him.
Perhaps it will not be long now,
A day, or two days, or a year,
Before he will understand that there is no building heaven,
Except it be thrust and locked and grounded on the granite of
 earth.

(Reprinted March 2, 1923, and June 15, 1923)

Everybody has been brought up to believe that money is really the most important thing in life. The business man justifies himself by that attitude. Our whole worship of success, or rather, financial success, is based upon it. The tremendous contrast between the things which are taught in the churches and the lives of the people is occasioned because of this dual standard. . . . One can always think what one likes, if one is willing to take the consequences. But I still maintain that this constant thinking about money, and not, say, real value about ordinary necessities, is what makes our life so distorted and queer. Why think about stupid things when there are ideas anywhere in the world? Ideas are the only really important things, you know, beside pine trees and books and art and people who are really themselves.

(December 2, 1922)

It is strange how quickly the humdrum minds of every day people lose that gem-like flame that is the eager life of being a child. Then every day is a

new adventure and the whole scope of the world, which one can touch and see and taste and smell and learn is an expansion of one's being, so that, with such a mind, the child is really the possessor of a life so full and rich and varied and beautiful that no riches of his adult days can equal it, and no hoarding of dear-bought memories can compensate for its loss. The whole world of color and light and movement is then the child's province. His life reaches everything, touches everything, is denied to nothing, hampered by nothing. Except as the years close in around him and he begins to shut himself off, here a little, there a little, hiding this wound, warding off that contact, until as he grows older the world which was his plaything becomes his narrow prison and he grows lonely and chilled, having stripped himself, until at the last he is in turn stripped, and the bare bones of him are hidden in the dust. A gloomy picture enough, and true enough. And yet how dreadfully unnecessary. Not that death is unnecessary, since we know it for what it is, a good release outward, but the narrowness, the shutting out of this world. The child is a great figure, a rich and full and powerful one because he includes the whole world in his zest and appreciation. But the adult who has shut himself off from the world has really strangled his world, shut himself in with sterility, and by building walls, has destroyed beauty.

A period of sterility has fallen on the world in the last fifty years. It is a sterility under which our lives and our art struggle in vain. Because the thing which has fallen upon our minds is the sense that everything is finished, that there is no hope, that human nature never can be changed, that idealism is a soap bubble, and that the only way of getting things is to fight and kill for them. Out of that sterility nothing good can come until we see how stupid and dull and miserable that way of thinking is, until we recognize that the permanent values are not those of money, but of right relation to the great whole. What a man is, in the whole scheme of things, must be more important than the money he has in the bank, the steam yachts he owns or the acreage of his real estate. And that is the thing that is coming.

It is a thing beyond religion. It is a thing beyond politics. It is a thing beyond the panaceas of professional uplifters and reformers. It is a great wind of new thinking which is coming upon the world. It is a new way of breaking down the walls which we adults have set up around us, with zest

and happiness and beauty and comradeship and the whole great world on the other side. It is a way of including them in us.

(February 11, 1923)

"The World Well Lost for Love."

It sings and battles and advances.
 As the sun beats above,
In spite of all the old romances.
 "The world well lost for love,"

Their faded pages mildewed over,
 With hearts and mourning doves,
There's no one now to weep the lover,
 Who lost the world for love.

We lose our loves, new year, old story,
 But still with high hearts move,
Exultant in the world's vast glory
 That's lovelier than love.

(April 3, 1923)

It is not at all a kind thing to do, but somehow we cannot help connecting the attitude of mind of the people who have allowed the convict system to go on in Florida and are now shocked by the investigation into Martin Tabert's death, with the attitude of the people who are now seeking to put a bill through the legislature to stop all teaching which shall in any way lead to Darwin. It is the same ostrich attitude of mind. A thing must not be true, they think, because they do not like to think it is true. And that is a very bad state of mind, indeed. It is the state of mind which persecuted the first man to believe that the earth was round and it is the state of mind which would willingly put a blight on all programs, for the sake of maintaining its own opinion. It does not believe in the rightness of the truth, whatever that may be proved to be. If the Florida legislature passes this bill it will make Florida a laughing stock as well as a state already shamed in the eyes of the country at large. It really is a little too much to be expected to bear cheerfully.

Funny about Darwin. They will stick to this monkey theory, which is not the true theory of Darwin at all, and completely ignore the greatest beliefs of that astonishing man of science, which were that the greatest factors in man's evolution have been the moral law and the ability to co-operate. The best arguments for the social tenets of their religion they decry daily as harmful. What a world, ye gods, what a world.

(April 27, 1923)

It would be a good thing if we could erase those words "altruism" and "philanthropy" from our speech. It is not thinking of others that we need. We need that finer and sounder attitude of mind which thinks of itself not first, but in its relation to the whole and which has the sheer common sense to see that the welfare of the whole is the finest thing to work for because it inevitably means more benefit to the individual than selfishness or altruism could possibly achieve.

See how the environment is really part and parcel of the individual. We cannot escape from it. From birth to death it colors our existence, shapes our minds, determines our living. Not just physical environment either, but people; the group of people with whom we are associated, the larger group beyond that, and so on, until the individual is really never for a moment isolated, as the old-fashioned way of thinking had him, but merely the unit of a constantly widening association.

When men see that more clearly they will understand why living has not been very much of a success. They will cease to struggle so much for their personal aggrandizement. They will recognize that a greater wealth will be theirs, a wider fame, if the community in which they function is richer in every sense, is more famous in every sense. And I mean by that rich in the ordered and beautiful ways of living and in fame for stimulated minds, free personalities and for greater opportunities for growth.

(May 6, 1923)

There is no question in the minds of thinking people that, after the turmoil and chaos of war, we are standing at the threshold of a new era. For the first time in human history we are seeing that the new era is not a thing which

will descend upon us in spite of ourselves, but a new attitude of mind to-
ward the whole people. We are bringing to bear on the problem of human
relations not the "let it alone" policy of the nineteenth century, not the
vague ethical feelings of duty to our fellow men or that sweetly sentimental
idea of "service," but the better understanding of after-the-war twentieth
century which recognizes that man is a related, not an isolated being,
whose living is so closely knotted and interwoven with the life of the whole
that only by this social understanding of himself can he help himself. His
will, which may reach its highest expression only through the social will, is
a creative thing. And it is a creative thing, for until men live in their own
group and then learn to think socially they cannot bring about a social will.
What the world needs is to find out how to create the common will, which
is the only way of democracy. What the twentieth century is beginning to
bring to us is the desire, the will, to create the common will.

(May 7, 1923)

It is the difference between the crowd and the group. We have, up till re-
cently, called any coming together of man in a mass, a crowd. We have said
that crowd psychology was a more primitive thing than individual psychol-
ogy. But we must begin to realize that man does function in his group and
that the psychology of the group may easily be a higher thing than the psy-
chology of the individual. Not crowd emotion, but group thinking, often
governs him. So that it is to the group process and our proper understand-
ing of it, to which we must turn for a way of learning how to live with one
another, how to create true democracy.

There is nothing more stimulating, nothing better fun, than to experi-
ence this group mind in action. It does not mean fight and it does not
mean compromise. There is no sense of imposed will. It becomes a true act
of creation if all members of that committee are actively interested in its
creation, if they are really wishing for the best thing, instead of working for
their own thing. The result is not a lot of different ideas, but one supremely
practicable, workable idea, the true group idea. But the people who pro-
duce that must come together willing to have it so. They must desire, not
their own, but the group spirit.

The group idea really means the bringing out of the best qualities of men's minds, instead of the crowd ideas, which is merely emotion. The ideal of the true group stimulates, while that of the crowd lowers and depresses. And when the individuals who go to make up the group, club, institution, organization, neighborhood or what not, really come together for the creation of an idea, by the method, not of imposed opinions, but of inter-stimulated thought, then we really have that thing which the founders of the republic believed was the basis of good government, the judgment of man raised to the highest power of which it is yet capable.

(May 10, 1923)

That newly formed League to Prevent Suicide has our hearty commendation and cooperation if they will take immediate steps to suppress all phonograph playing before seven o'clock in the morning and the people who call you up on the telephone and say, "Who is this?"

(June 23, 1923)

Epilogue

Douglas wrote her last column for the *Herald*'s July 31, 1923, issue. The strain of meeting a daily deadline had taken its toll, and her doctor recommended that she leave the newspaper. The last Galley offered neither parting words of farewell nor even a suggestion that the finale had come. Yet when viewed in the context of her later life, the column makes a fitting conclusion for the woman whose name would become synonymous with the Everglades. It is pleasingly prophetic that the last passage of the last Galley reveals Douglas's inquisitive nature in ponderings related to the Everglades and the Miami River. Twenty years later, author Hervey Allen approached Douglas to write a book on the Miami River for the Rivers of America series, which he was editing for Rinehart and Company. Douglas suggested instead a book about the Everglades, the river of grass.

∽∽

It is undoubtedly true that the farther west you go away from the waterfront, the cooler it gets. I don't see why, really. Perhaps that is a phenomenon for weather men to explain. But certainly you can come in from the sea where it has been lovely with a great salt wind, and still go west toward the Everglades and notice a marked drop in temperature. All around the [Miami] river it is cooler, too. You can feel the difference as you approach it. It is as if there were always a great current of cooler air rushing up the river and cooling off both banks, but especially reaching across Riverside with a great wing of cool air. Then out beyond, out where the vast wideness of the Everglades opens on each side, you can find roads where the air is almost chilly at night, wet and chilly, with a tang in it and the fresh clean smell of

acres of green growing things silent under the stars. Is it because the waters of the bay are shallow and so retain the warmth more, and that farther west they get the sea winds from higher up, or what? We have always been curious.

Notes

Editor's Note: In these notes, Marjory Stoneman Douglas is referred to as "MSD," and the Marjory Stoneman Douglas Papers at the University of Miami are cited as "MSD Papers."

Introduction

1. Cathy Shaw, "The Friend of the Everglades," *Wellesley Magazine,* Summer 1983, 14–16; Joseph Podgor, Interview, Miami Springs, Fla., August 10, 2000.

2. MSD Papers, Otto G. Richter Library, University of Miami, Coral Gables, Fla., Special Collections and Archives Department, Clippings File, Box 39. MSD, "Alumnae Achievement Award," *Wellesley Alumnae Magazine,* Spring 1977, 31.

3. On Douglas's life in general, see MSD with John Rothchild, *Marjory Stoneman Douglas: Voice of the River* (Sarasota: Pineapple Press, 1987).

4. Helen Muir, Interview, Miami, March 11, 1999.

5. Kevin McCarthy has collected a number of Douglas's short stories. See his *Nine Florida Stories by Marjory Stoneman Douglas* (Jacksonville: University of North Florida Press, 1990); and *"A River in Flood" and Other Florida Stories by Marjory Stoneman Douglas* (Gainesville: University Press of Florida, 1998).

6. "He Man," published in the *Saturday Evening Post,* July 30, 1927, was named one of the O. Henry Memorial Award Prize Stories of 1927; and "The Peculiar Treasures of Kings," ibid., November 26, 1927, won second place from the O. Henry Memorial Award Committee for the best short story by an American writer published in an American magazine. Doubleday, Doran and Co., Garden City, N.Y., to Marjory Stoneman Douglas, November 26, 1928, and "For Excellent Short Story," MSD Papers, undated clipping, folder 44, box 33; Rosalie E. Leposky, "Marjory Stoneman Douglas Bibliography," *Marjory Kinnan Rawlings Journal of Florida Literature* 8 (1997): 55–73; McCarthy, *Nine Stories,* xi.

7. Jeffrey Meyers, *Scott Fitzgerald: A Biography* (New York: Harper Collins,

1994); MSD Papers, memo, "Her Short Stories," n.d., folder 12, box 39; George Horace Lorimer to MSD, April 7, 1927, folder 10, box 54.

8. On Douglas's early life, see MSD, *Voice of the River.*

9. On the subject of Populism, see Richard Hofstadter, *The Age of Reform: From Bryan to F.D.R.* (New York: Alfred A. Knopf, 1968); Lawrence Goodwynn, *Democratic Promise: The Populist Moment in America* (New York: Oxford University Press, 1976). On William Jennings Bryan, see Robert W. Cherny, *Righteous Cause: The Life of William Jennings Bryan* (Boston: Little, Brown, 1985).

10. On the subject of Progressivism, see Hofstadter, *Age of Reform;* Robert W. Wiebe, *The Search for Order, 1877–1920* (New York: Oxford University Press, 1968); Dewey Grantham, *Southern Progressivism: The Reconciliation of Progress and Tradition* (Knoxville: University of Tennessee Press, 1983).

11. Taunton (Mass.) High School, *The Journal and Stylus* (1908), 19, Taunton Public Library.

12. Marjory Stoneman, "An Early Morning Paddle," *Boston Herald,* June 23, 1907.

13. Marjory Stoneman, "The Tree Day Pageant at Wellesley," MSD Papers, box 41, file 38.

14. MSD, "Perspectives," *Wellesley Alumnae Magazine,* Summer 1977: 22.

15. MSD, "Alumnae Achievement Award," 31.

16. MSD, "Frank Bryant Stoneman," *Tequesta,* November 1944, 7–8; MSD Papers, untitled manuscript by MSD, n.d., folder 123, box 48; MSD, *Voice of the River,* 41–83.

17. MSD, "Alumnae Achievement Award," 31; MSD, "Frank Bryant Stoneman"; MSD, untitled manuscript; MSD, *Voice of the River,* 41–92.

18. Raymond A. Mohl, "Miami: The Ethnic Cauldron," in *Sunbelt Cities: Politics and Growth Since World War II,* ed. Richard M. Bernard and Bradley R. Rice (Austin: University of Texas Press, 1983), 59; Edward N. Akin, *Flagler: Rockefeller Partner and Florida Baron* (Kent, OH: Kent State University Press, 1988); John Wilborn Martin, *Henry Flagler (1830–1913): Florida's East Coast Is His Monument!* (n.p., n.d.); Helen Muir, *Miami U.S.A.* (Gainesville: University Press of Florida, 2000).

19. MSD, "Frank Bryant Stoneman," 5; Doris Ritzinger to MSD, July 14, 1952, MSD Papers, folder 78, box 44.

20. Helen Muir, Interview.

21. MSD, *Voice of the River,* 37.

22. MSD to Dorothy Vaile, July 18, 1985, MSD Papers, folder 78, box 44; Leon F. Litwack, *North of Slavery: The Negro in the Free States, 1790–1860* (Chicago: University of Chicago Press, 1961), 12–13; MSD, "Levi Coffin's Road to Freedom," MSD Papers, manuscript, folder 113, box 47.

23. MSD, *Voice of the River,* 100.

24. MSD, "Frank Bryant Stoneman," 11.

25. MSD, *Voice of the River,* 102.

26. MSD to May Mann Jennings, December 2, 1917, May Mann Jennings Papers, Correspondence, box 12, P. K. Yonge Library, University of Florida, Gainesville.

27. Linda D. Vance, *May Mann Jennings: Florida's Genteel Activist* (Gainesville: University Press of Florida, 1985), 95.

28. Jeffrey Meyers, *Hemingway: A Biography* (New York: Da Capo Press, 1999).

29. See for instance, MSD, "The Hand Is Quicker," *Saturday Evening Post,* March 5, 1938: 12.

30. *Miami Herald,* December 27, 1920.

31. On women in journalism, see Marion Marzolf, *Up From the Footnote: A History of Women Journalists* (New York: Hastings House, 1977); Nan Robertson, *The Girls in the Balcony: Women, Men, and the New York Times* (New York: Random House, 1992); Robert C. Kochersberger, *More Than a Muckraker: Ida Tarbell's Lifetime in Journalism* (Knoxville: University of Tennessee Press, 1994).

32. For the prevailing attitudes toward the environment in the early twentieth century, see Samuel P. Hays, *Conservation and the Gospel of Efficiency: The Progressive Conservation Movement, 1890–1920* (New York: Atheneum, 1969); Roderick Nash, *Wilderness and the American Mind* (New Haven, Conn.: Yale University Press, 1982).

33. Unfortunately for Douglas, the poem "Nocturne," initially accepted by *Scribner's Magazine,* was rejected when the magazine, which had a policy against using previously published work, learned that the poem had been printed in the *Miami Herald* (Charles Scribner's Sons to M. S. Douglas, July 27 and August 3, 1920, MSD Papers, box 40, file 17).

34. All in MSD Papers, box 40: George to Marjorie [*sic*] S. Douglas, September 28, 1920, file 17; John E. Holland to MSD, April 22, 1922, file 14; Mary P. Gould to MSD, September 29, 1920, file 17.

35. Diary, December 9, 1924–June 16, 1925, MSD Papers, box 27.

36. David McCally, *The Everglades: An Environmental History* (Gainesville: University Press of Florida, 1999); Mark S. Foster, *Castles in the Sand: The Life and Times of Carl Graham Fisher* (Gainesville: University Press of Florida, 2000).

Chapter 1. Nature Lover

1. Douglas spent thirty years working on the Hudson biography but never published it. Versions of the manuscript can be found in her papers at the Richter library at the University of Miami.

2. Typos and misspellings found in the original newspaper copy have been corrected for the benefit of reading clarity.

Chapter 2. South Florida Booster

1. MSD, "Alumnae Achievement Award," 31.

2. Shaw, "The Friend of the Everglades," 16.

3. Merrill Jensen, ed., *Regionalism in America* (Madison: University of Wisconsin Press, 1965); Daniel Joseph Singal, *The War Within: From Victorian to Modernist Thought in the South, 1919–1945* (Chapel Hill: University of North Carolina Press, 1982), 148–52.

4. See Hays, *Conservation and the Gospel of Efficiency.*

5. Foster, *Castles in the Sand.*

6. MSD, untitled manuscript, 29.

7. David Fairchild was a good friend of Douglas. He was an entomologist living in Coral Gables who brought scores of exotic plants from around the world to South Florida. The gardens he and his wife, Marian, created from these and other plants became Fairchild Gardens, which are now open to the public.

Chapter 3. Political Analyst

1. See David R. Colburn and Lance deHaven-Smith, *Government in the Sunshine: Florida Since Statehood* (Gainesville: University Press of Florida, 1999).

2. Hofstadter, *Age of Reform;* Wiebe, *Search for Order;* Grantham, *Southern Progressivism.*

3. Debs opposed American intervention in the war in Europe, and was arrested in 1918 and given a twenty-year prison sentence for encouraging draft resistance. During the 1920 presidential election, while still behind bars, Debs polled close to one million votes.

4. Many localities had laws, known as blue laws, that restricted certain types of business, work, and social activities on Sundays.

5. As head of the Food Administration, created during the war to keep the Allied countries and soldiers fed, Hoover organized the Belgian Relief, a massive aid program to feed war-torn European countries.

6. During the campaign for the presidency in 1920, Warren G. Harding referred to "normalcy," a non-word at the time, instead of "normality." To the chagrin of purists, his mistake resulted in the addition of a new word to American English.

7. Once a territory of Germany, the Pacific island of Yap was mandated by the League of Nations to Japan.

8. In the fall of 1919, Wilson suffered a stroke that left him partially paralyzed.

9. A province on the border of Hungary.

Chapter 4. Woman

1. MSD, "Alumnae Achievement Award," 31.

2. It is uncertain whether these are the words of MSD or of another writer she was quoting. See "The Fighting Lady," Diary, Aug. 1–Dec. 8, 1924, MSD Papers, box 27.

Chapter 5. Social Progressive

1. Mercedes M. Randall, *Improper Bostonian: Emily Greene Balch* (New York: Twayne Publishers, 1946); Cindy Miller, "Marjory Stoneman Douglas spurs 'grassroots,'" MSD Papers, clipping, folder 11, box 39; MSD, *Voice of the River,* 76.

2. On Florida convict leasing, see Jerrell H. Shofner, "Postscript to the Martin Tabert Case: Peonage as Usual in the Florida Turpentine Camps," *Florida Historical Quarterly* 60 (1981), 164–66; Jerrell H.Schofner, "Forced Labor in Florida Forests, 1880–1950," *Journal of Forest History* 25 (1981): 18–20; J. C. Powell, *The American Siberia; or, Fourteen Years Experience in a Southern Convict Camp* (Chicago: Donohue, Henneberry, 1891); on the subject in the South, see Pete Daniel, *The Shadow of Slavery: Peonage in the South* (Urbana: University of Illinois Press, 1972).

3. The American Civil Liberties Union of Greater Miami, the first ACLU affiliate organized below the Mason-Dixon line, was chartered in 1955. The charter application, dated July 22, 1955, in Dade County, is preserved in the American Civil Liberties Union of Florida Records, folder 1, box 1, P. K. Yonge Library, University of Florida, Gainesville.

4. Frank H. "Hard-Boiled" Smith was a lieutenant in the Military Police in Paris during World War I. He had a reputation for being excessively rough with doughboys and was eventually court-martialed and sentenced for brutality.

5. Ford was a prominent anti-Semite who sponsored a publicity campaign against Jews.

6. Catt was a leader in the women's suffrage movement.

7. A social reform movement of the late nineteenth and twentieth centuries, eugenics called for the improved health and intelligence of offspring. Some eugenics reformers embraced eugenics as a way to rid society of "undesirable" groups, such as the poor and racial minorities.

8. Hookworm plagued the population of the South, especially the rural poor,

and other tropical and subtropical regions of the Western Hemisphere. In 1914, hookworm infected 39 percent of the children tested in the South. Florida was the first southern state to launch a a campaign against hookworm.

9. In 1903, Florida became the first southern state to establish a bacteriological laboratory to deal with the problem of tuberculosis.

Chapter 6. Intellectual

1. Joseph Podgor, Interview; Michael Chenowith, Interview, Miami, August 9, 2000; Franklin Adams, Interview, Naples, Fla., August 9, 2000.

2. Douglas's father was among those who believed that Bacon was the true author of Shakespeare's work.

3. Wilson held a Ph.D. from Johns Hopkins and was a published and well-respected political science professor and historian at Princeton and president of Princeton University before becoming governor of New Jersey and president of the United States.

4. During the campaign for the presidency in 1920, Warren G. Harding referred to "normalcy," a non-word at the time, instead of "normality." To the chagrin of vocabulary purists, his mistake resulted in the addition of a new word to American English.

Chapter 7. Philosopher and Observer of Human Nature

1. MSD, *Voice of the River,* 257.

2. MSD, "Perspectives," 22.

3. Douglas was likely quoting the cockroach free-verse poet Archy in Don Marquis's Archy and Mehitabel stories, popular in the early twentieth century. Late at night, Archy would leave notes on Marquis's typewriter, always in lower-case, waxing philosophical about his insect world and his companion Mehitabel, a cynical cat in her ninth life. Clearly, Archy was inspiration for Douglas's own Gustavas Adolphus, a mouse who would type out messages in lower-case letters to the "galley slave." See pages 184–85.

Jack E. Davis is associate professor of history and director of environmental studies at the University of Alabama at Birmingham. The author of *Race Against Time: Culture and Separation in Natchez Since 1930* (2001), he is currently at work on a biography of Marjory Stoneman Douglas.

The Florida History and Culture Series
Edited by Raymond Arsenault and Gary R. Mormino

Al Burt's Florida: Snowbirds, Sand Castles, and Self-Rising Crackers, by Al Burt (1997)

Black Miami in the Twentieth Century, by Marvin Dunn (1997)

Gladesmen: Gator Hunters, Moonshiners, and Skiffers, by Glen Simmons and Laura Ogden (1998)

"Come to My Sunland": Letters of Julia Daniels Moseley from the Florida Frontier, 1882–1886, by Julia Winifred Moseley and Betty Powers Crislip (1998)

The Enduring Seminoles: From Alligator Wrestling to Ecotourism, by Patsy West (1998)

Government in the Sunshine State: Florida Since Statehood, by David R. Colburn and Lance deHaven-Smith (1999)

The Everglades: An Environmental History, by David McCally (1999)

Beechers, Stowes, and Yankee Strangers: The Transformation of Florida, by John T. Foster, Jr., and Sarah Whitmer Foster (1999)

The Tropic of Cracker, by Al Burt (1999)

Balancing Evils Judiciously: The Proslavery Writings of Zephaniah Kingsley, edited and annotated by Daniel W. Stowell (1999)

Hitler's Soldiers in the Sunshine State: German POWs in Florida, by Robert D. Billinger, Jr. (2000)

Cassadaga: The South's Oldest Spiritualist Community, edited by John J. Guthrie, Phillip Charles Lucas, and Gary Monroe (2000)

Claude Pepper and Ed Ball: Politics, Purpose, and Power, by Tracy E. Danese (2000)

Pensacola during the Civil War: A Thorn in the Side of the Confederacy, by George F. Pearce (2000)

Castles in the Sand: The Life and Times of Carl Graham Fisher, by Mark S. Foster (2000)

Miami, U.S.A., by Helen Muir (2000)

Politics and Growth in Twentieth-Century Tampa, by Robert Kerstein (2001)

The Invisible Empire: The Ku Klux Klan in Florida, by Michael Newton (2001)

The Wide Brim: Early Poems and Ponderings of Marjory Stoneman Douglas, edited by Jack E. Davis (2002)